THIS IS JUST MY FACE

TRY NOT TO STARE

GABOUREY SIDIBE

• • •

HARPER**AVENUE**

Published by Harper Avenue,
an imprint of HarperCollins Publishers Ltd

First Canadian edition

HarperCollins Publishers Ltd
2 Bloor Street East, 20th Floor
Toronto, Ontario, Canada
M4W 1A8

www.harpercollins.ca

Library and Archives Canada Cataloguing in Publication information
is available upon request.

ISBN 978-1-44344-937-3

Book design by Kelly Dubeau Smydra

Jacket Photography © Guzman
Jacket Styling: Wardrobe by Marcy Guevara, Hair by Chuck Amos,
Makeup by Cassandra Garcia, Props by Eleventh Street Workshop,
Dress by Grass Fields, and Couch by Mbenga Akinnagbe

Printed and bound in the United States of America

LSC/H 10 9 8 7 6 5 4 3 2 1

CONTENTS

THIS IS JUST MY FACE

1

CLAW-FOOT TUB AND MERMAID TAIL

Leave Gabby alone. She's pretty . . . in her own way.

— like every girl in my seventh-grade class

HALLOWEEN NIGHT A YEAR AGO. I hadn't been home for months, so when my favorite friend, Kia, said to me, "Boo! GO TO BED! Put your phone in the guest bathroom and take yo ass to sleep!" I knew she was right. Our friendship started on the film *Precious*. Kia was the production assistant who was mostly in charge of babysitting me. Years later, she has become one of my best friends, my producing partner, and one of the people who knows me better than I know myself. Like right now when she knows that even though I say I'm fine I'm not. Truth is, I was tired. I didn't want to run around the city drunk. The e-mail I'd just received said . . . shit, two days, and I had to fly out again. I'd have barely enough time to see my mom and my brother, and have brunch with my Main Gay.

The tough thing about staying in on Halloween is seeing all the tweets, instagrams, and texts from people cooler than I am who are all dressed up and out partying. This is more fun for them than it is for me because they don't get to dress up for a living like I do—this is what I was trying to convince myself, but it wasn't working. Dressing up is *still* really fun for me. I heard my phone buzz. I should've put it in the bathroom like Kia suggested but . . . I'm not addicted to my phone or anything . . . you are! Shut up! Anyway, among the pictures of slutty outfits showing up on my feed were texts from friends saying, "What do you mean you're staying in? Come out with us, you whore!" There were also a few pictures and videos of people dressed up as Precious for Halloween. Precious, the character I'd played in my first-ever film. The character who people seemed to think that it was hilarious to confuse with me . . . ME.

Someone sent a picture featuring a black man wearing jeans and a sweater. He had a pillow under his shirt and more pillows down his legs so he looked both pregnant and fat. His face was made up so he appeared to be even darker than he already was—the almost-never-seen blacker blackface. In one hand he held a composition notebook and in the other an empty bucket of fried chicken as his props. He was standing next to a black woman in a gray jogging suit smoking a cigarette and holding a skillet as if it were a bat. Mary, Precious's mother. Hilarious.

When I was in the fourth grade, I borrowed an evening gown from my mother and went trick or treating dressed as

Scarlett O'Hara from *Gone with the Wind*. Never did I think, ever, that one day people would dress up as me for Halloween. What an honor, right?

But I didn't feel honored. I felt offended. So offended that I planned to ignore for the next few weeks the "friends" who'd sent me those pictures. (I'm very organized in my pettiness, and I like to plan ahead.)

Here's the thing: what offends me is not that people are dressing up as *me*. I know they're just dressing up as a character I played. That character is iconic in her way and probably means more to the people dressing up as her than she means to me. I am really clear about the fact that, while I *played* Precious, she's not me. We may have the same face and body, but we stand for two completely different things. Precious is a survivor, and I refuse to be anyone's survivor because I prefer to think of myself as a winner. So even though the blacker blackfaces and fat-pillow costumes hit me like a skillet in the face, that's actually beside the point here. I can understand that the average viewer might see them as homage, fantasy, authenticity. My beef isn't with them; it's with my friends who are laughing at the costumes and wanting me to laugh with them. My beef is with feeling forced to have a sense of humor about what I look like. *Well, I don't fucking feel like it.*

Before I met Lee Daniels, who cast and directed me in the role of Precious, my life was very different. Meeting him set off a domino effect so strong that I can very easily trace the life I'm living—typing in my MacBook in my Upper West Side apartment—back to him. Every yes I get in my life from now on will be because he said yes first. He was the first man ever to say, "You're beautiful, and here's what we're going to do with it." He's done more for me than my own father. He's taught me more with grunts than any teacher has ever taught me with words. All of his compliments feel like heaven, and all of his negative comments feel like a thousand knives to my gut. (I often tell him that what I feel for him is Stockholm syndrome.)

One day while I was sitting around waiting for *Precious* to come out so that I could finally tell everyone who'd ever been mean to me that they could suck it, Lee called. He told me that his friend André Leon Talley had just seen a screening of the film for the third time, and he loved it. And he loved me! I had no idea who André Leon Talley was, but Lee seemed super excited so I opened my computer to look him up while Lee went on and on.

"Oh, that's so cool!" I said, pretending to know exactly what was happening.

"You don't know who that is, do you?" Lee asked.

I wasn't typing fast enough.

"No, but I'm still really excited! Is he your buddy?"

"No, dummy! Well, yes! He's *Vogue,* Miss Honey! HE IS *VOGUE!* He is EVERYTHING! He wants to put you on the cover!"

By then I had "American editor-at-large for *Vogue* magazine . . . contributing editor . . . front-row regular at fashion shows in New York, Paris, London and Milan for more than 25 years" up on Wikipedia. Turns out, he's a legend! My ignorance about him could only be explained by the fact that I am ignorant of most things *fashion.*

My response: "Aww, shit . . . cool!"

I was still putting together what this meant. It was only just dawning on me that someone could want me on the cover of *any* magazine, let alone *Vogue.* Holy hell! Those people who'd been mean to me were *really* going to suffer now.

"Hello? Gabby? Girl, it's *VOGUE,*" Lee yelled into the phone.

Finally, I yelled back, "Oh, my God! Really?? Me!?"

This was the response he was looking for.

"Yes! YOU, Gabbala! YOU! He's crazy about you. He loves the film. LOVES IT. You're a star now, Gabby. A star!" Lee's words were pumping my ego with oxygen.

I'd had too little to do after *Precious* was filmed and before it was released. Sitting around and knowing that something *good* was coming was just as unnerving for me as sitting around and feeling that something *bad* was coming. It drove me nuts. I'd be excited one minute and then depressed the next. I'd wait for calls from Lee to remind me that I wasn't a loser — that I was a winner and that something good was coming for me soon. This was one of those calls.

"I'm a star!" I yelled back.

I only half believed my own statement. It was still an insane notion that I was anybody's star. But as long as Lee had said it first, it started to feel like the truth.

"That's right, kid! I have a ton of things to discuss with you, so come over and meet me at my apartment."

"When?"

"Right now! Get over here."

I truly lived for these moments during what seemed like a forever-long wait for that film to come out. I was on a train headed over to his apartment in less than ten minutes.

The entire way to Lee's, I was super excited that a fashion bigwig I'd never heard of wanted to put me on the cover of this exclusive magazine. I fantasized about how fun my *Vogue* photo shoot would be. I imagined myself dressed as a mermaid lounging in an empty claw-foot tub, a long string of pearls hanging around my neck and twirled around the fingers of my left hand. My smiling face would be resting on the back of my right hand while my elbow would perch on the edge of the tub. My hair would be blowing up and away from my face for that Ariel/Beyoncé look. My purple and turquoise tail fins would caress the edge of the tub. The floor and the walls would be gold, and a beautiful red-satin shower curtain would be pulled open to reveal the wonder that is me. ME! Large diamonds would be strewn about the floor. Why on the floor? Because I'd be so rich that I'd be careless with my things.

By the time I got to Lee's building, I had come up with the perfect headline for my cover. At this point, I'd been at Lee's place so often that I just waved to security as I entered the elevator. On the way up, I saw it all forming above my head in big letters. The headline would read: "Gabourey Sidibe. You Should've Been Nicer to Her," and then *Vogue* in smaller letters under my name or, ya know, wherever they could fit it.

Often I would get off the elevator at Lee's floor to the sound of his disco music pumping through his closed door, or I'd hear him yelling excitedly to someone about one of his films. This time I heard a big voice over speakerphone shrieking, "That fat bitch is going on the cover!" The words were coming from Lee's apartment, and they sliced right through my fantasy. I froze where I was.

"You hear me, Lee? I'm putting that fat bitch right on the cover of *Vogue*. I love her. That black bitch WILL be on the cover!" André yelled.

"YES!!!! She is EVERYTHING!" Lee screeched in agreement.

"I don't care what I have to do, I'm putting that fat bitch on the cover!"

They cackled together and made plans for me and my fat ass and the cover. Not the cover of just any magazine, but *Vogue*. I stood silently. I was sneaking in on a conversation I wasn't meant to hear about sneaking into a world I wasn't meant to be a part of. Not feeling horrible, but no longer feeling super excited, I waited for it to be over.

I'd been called a fat bitch before. I'd been called a fat black bitch before. But this was different. André loved me in the film, loved my performance, and wanted to put me on the cover of his magazine. But I was still a fat bitch. A fat black bitch.

I knew what I looked like. I had mirrors in my home. I'd seen myself in pictures. I wasn't in the dark about it. I just assumed at the time that if I could display a talent worthy of praise, if I could prove that I was worthy of attention, that I wasn't just who you thought I was . . . I guess I thought I wouldn't be fat anymore. That may seem silly. I know that now. But at the time I thought that if I could just get the world to see me the way I saw myself then my body wouldn't be the thing you walked away thinking about. I wouldn't be that fat girl. I wouldn't be that dark-skinned girl. I'd be Gabby. I'd be human.

I thought that starring in a movie would change that. Shouldn't it? Wouldn't being on the cover of a magazine change that? But how could it if the very person putting me on the cover was the person calling me a fat black bitch behind my back? They'd all be nice to my face, but it was dawning on me that they'd still have their private opinions, that I was still too fat and still too black. The world wasn't different just because I'd made a movie.

I was different. Maybe that needed to be enough.

Lee and André finished their conversation, and I got back on the elevator and went down to ask security to buzz me up as if I'd just gotten there. A big part of me wanted a redo, to have missed hearing what I'd now never forget. Once I was in Lee's apartment, he greeted me excitedly. He told me that André had just called and that they were both so excited about what would become of me.

"Can you just DIE?! Can you believe it? YOU! On the cover of *Vogue!* I'm gagging." He was just as excited as before. He didn't say anything about André calling me a fat black bitch, and I didn't say anything about hearing him do it. Lee hadn't called me a fat bitch, but he hadn't defended me. Though I wasn't sure what he could've said to defend me. I am fat and black, and often I refer to myself as a bitch. Where's the lie? How do you defend that? He preferred to celebrate.

"YES! I'm gagging! I'm so excited!" I answered.

I wasn't sure if I should admit to what I heard. And if I did, I wasn't sure I was allowed to feel offended anymore. Yes, André had called me a fat bitch a bunch (like one hundred times), but he'd also said he'd make me a cover girl. He'd said I was a star. How could I be offended? I should be grateful. There were plenty of fat black bitches out there who'd never be on the cover of a magazine. Also, André is a large black man in a position of power. How many times had he endured being called a fat black bitch? Both behind his back and to his face? More than enough, I'm sure. Maybe enough not only to turn that insult into a compliment but also enough to give it as a compliment as well. And wasn't it a compliment? What would it have meant to him to put me on the cover of *Vogue*? From one fat black bitch to another? Would that have been a win for *him*?

Perhaps I had to change my idea of what an insult sounds like. Was this insult the best compliment I could ever garner from the fashion industry (which would eventually call me and my body a "joke")? Had my eavesdropping helped me to stumble on an important message? One that said I should love the hate. Is this how you become a celebrity? *Don't be offended. Be glad they know who you are.*

Well, I just have to say: I was offended. When someone says something negative about me, it hurts my feelings. It always has, and it probably always will. It doesn't hurt as much as it did when I was younger, but it still hurts. I'll never feel glad that someone says something awful about me. I'll never bask in the negative attention. It's ridiculous that I'm asked to do so. I'm a fucking human being! I'm not weak. But I am human.

I don't think it's funny when people stuff pillows in their clothing to look like me. I don't think it's funny when people paint their faces to look like me. I don't think it's funny when a stranger calls me a fat bitch no matter what they're offering to do for me. I don't think it's funny that I'm not allowed to say that my feelings are hurt. Feelings aren't an absence of strength. I know this for sure. So why should I pretend to have a sense of humor just to allow someone else to take a shot at me?

People have their opinions about me. For now, their opinions are basically about my body. It seems as though if I cured cancer and won a Nobel Prize someone would say, "Sure, cancer sucks and I'm glad there's a cure, but her body is just disgusting. She needs to spend less time in the science lab and more time in the gym!" Even people who want to put me on the covers of magazines will wonder how much I eat or how I fit through a door. The best thing to do with those opinions is to ignore them and listen to my own. I could lose weight. That is a fact. But I am dope at any and every size. I am smart. I am funny. I am talented. I am gorgeous. I am black. I am fat. Sometimes I'm a bitch. At all times, I am a *bad bitch*. (The word *bitch* is pretty confusing, right?)

I have yet to grace the cover of *Vogue*. I guess they couldn't find a claw-foot tub big enough for me and my mermaid tail. I had to settle for being in the pages of *Vogue* in a CoverGirl feature instead. I still consider it a win for fat black bitches everywhere. André Leon Talley included.

2

VIRGIN FO' LIFE

Dude just DM'd me an unsolicited dick pic,
but his profile says, "Through God, all things
are possible"... I am very confused.

— my Twitter

MY MOM AND I ARE always discussing how we'd deal with attempted rape. Sometimes we decide that we'd fight tooth and nail. We'd bite our attacker in the dick; in our minds, the rapist is insistent on foreplay and surely wants to be pleasured orally. We bite his dick, he goes down in pain, and we run out of the house or down the alley screaming, blood dripping down the sides of our mouths. Other times we go along with all of our attacker's requests. We lull him into a false sense of security, and when he least expects it, we claw at his face and genitals, and then run out of the house or down the alley screaming, blood dripping from our fingernails. We are never together in the scenarios we envision. We can't imagine that an attacker would look at the two of us together and think *gangbang*. No. We are always alone, at home or getting on the subway very late at night.

I admit, my mom and I don't take into account the scenarios in which our strategies could get us killed. Nor do we ever consider being paralyzed by fear. But we are genuinely discussing how we envision ourselves fighting off an attack. Really, it's something that all mothers and daughters should discuss. The same way that all fathers and sons should discuss why no one should ever be raped in the first place. It's my theory that not enough fathers and sons discuss rape, and so my mother and I have to discuss it just about every time I go see her.

When I was twenty-seven, I went to visit my mom, who was still living in the apartment in Harlem I grew up in. I sat while she ran around the kitchen cooking food for me, getting a glass of tea for me, asking if there was something else she could do for me. She waits on me now because I'm a guest. My mother always makes such a huge fuss over me, and it makes me feel like an adult and a child at the same time. When I first moved out, I thought the apartment would feel like home as long as my family still lived there. Not the case. It's actually a huge disappointment to go back and feel like a visitor instead of like a daughter to my mother and a little sister to my brother. Everything feels smaller. The doorways are shorter, the toilet is closer to the ground, and I no longer know how to turn on the TV. I'm grown now.

So we were in the kitchen discussing rape, as usual, when my mother said, "You'd better really fight. It would be so hard on you because you're still a virgin, and that's not how you want to lose your virginity."

???

It was a total record-scratch moment! She called me a virgin, and she said it with sincerity and a touch of pity. Here I was, twenty-seven years old, having lived on my own for two years, and she just *knew for a fact* that I was a virgin. I even had a boyfriend at the time, and she still felt confident in her belief that I was a virgin — confident enough to bring it up as obvious in a conversation about a completely different subject. Well, she was wrong. I wasn't a virgin. I'm still not a virgin. That's right. I've gone all the way.

However, I *am* fascinated by virginity. Losing it, keeping it, only doing hand and mouth stuff because you regard your vag as a delicate little prize for your husband on your wedding night. Sacrificing your butt hole to save your porcelain-baby vagina from being smushed and crushed by some dude who barely knows what he's doing. Hey, girl, I get it! Kind of. Wait . . . no. I don't really get it, but I'm not here to judge you. Everyone has his or her reasons for holding on to it — until they don't. Frankly, that's the way it should be. Letting some dude put his stuff in you is actually pretty heavy. It's serious. But I didn't think about my virginity that way before I lost it. I didn't see it as a treasure or a precious jewel. I had felt the burden of my virginity ever since my friend, a guy, told me when I was sixteen that if I was still a virgin at twenty-one he'd do me a favor and take it from me. He said it out of nowhere! Like he was so sure that I was so undesirable that he'd have to go ahead and lie on the cross and take my virginity from me as an act of charity. Bless him. I couldn't think of anything sadder than being a pity fuck. That's not normal. I couldn't let it happen. I saw it as a burden that I had to get rid of so that I could be normal like my friends. A few years later, I looked around and I was the only virgin left and I basically panicked.

If you think that's a story I'm about to tell you, you're wrong. There is no story. I was twenty years old. I wasn't a child bride. I wasn't being forced, but I hadn't figured it out any more than my friends had. I just thought, *Well . . . that's enough*. And then *boom*, I wasn't a virgin anymore. And then came the regret. Not regret over losing my virginity — regret over my rush to do it. It had seemed so important that it had become a project for me. How would it happen? Who would it happen with? Where would it happen? Would I be a grown-up afterward? Would I suddenly become a sexy woman with a small waist, big boobs, and a big ass? Would I be Jessica Rabbit or Beyoncé? The answer was no. I didn't become any of those things, and the where, how, and who of it all left me disappointed as well.

Don't worry! At least I got the dude's full age and name beforehand. He didn't have a middle name, and I thought, *Wow. Your parents didn't love you enough to give you a middle name. What a shame*. And just to make sure I'd never have to see him again, I shared that thought with him.

He looked at me, and then he laughed. He thought I was funny. That was enough for me so I banged him.

Are you judging me? Remember, you were super shitty at twenty years old, possibly shittier than I was. You remember that!

For a while afterward, I kept trying to make sex feel good, but it didn't. Not with anyone. And I *really* tried. I'd go after guys who were very attractive, but they didn't feel any better than ugly guys. I'd try guys who really wanted to be in a relationship with me, but they didn't feel any better than the guys just looking for something to do on a Friday night. I tried to make a game out of it. I'd try on a character to see if she had more fun, but she did not. I kept thinking that the problem was each individual guy. Like I said, I really tried. But it always felt the same. Cold. Emotionless. Empty.

This was a very strange time in my life. I was slipping into a depression, and while I didn't super love sex, every encounter at least became something I could focus on to distract me from the fact that I was severely unhappy with everything in my life.

I didn't see it then, but that phase of pseudopromiscuity was a part of my depression, not a distraction from it. Poor, stupid, slutty Gabby. To be clear, it wasn't a lot of men. It was a few. This is what I did, though, off and on between the ages of twenty and twenty-two. I call it my Hoe Phase.

Here's the thing about therapy and why it is so important. I love my mom, but there's so much I couldn't talk to her about during my Hoe Phase. I couldn't tell her that I couldn't stop crying and that I hated everything about myself. My mom has always been an independent person with lots of friends who love her and think she is the most talented person ever. Her life at the age of twenty was nothing like mine. Whenever I did try to open up, my mom seemed unconcerned. When I was sad about something, she told me to "get a thicker skin"; when I was upset, she told me to "stop nitpicking." My mom has always had faith that things would be okay—but saying "Tomorrow will be a better day" wasn't enough for me. When I first told her I was depressed, she laughed. Literally. Not because she's a terrible person, but because she thought it was a joke. How could I not be able to feel better on my own—like her, like her friends, like normal people?

So I just kept thinking my sad thoughts. Thoughts about dying. I couldn't sleep at night. Eventually, morning would come, and it would be time to go to class. I was attending City College of New York, a five-minute walk from my apartment, but by the time I'd get to school every morning, I'd be crying and sweating profusely, struggling to breathe, thinking I was going to die. For a while, I thought I was having asthma attacks. I didn't realize until later that these were actually panic attacks. I was a mess.

I stopped eating. For days at a time, I wouldn't eat anything at all. Often, when I was too sad to stop crying, I drank a glass of water and ate a slice of bread, and then I threw it up. After I did, I wasn't as sad anymore. I finally relaxed. So I never ate anything until I wanted to throw up, and only when I did could I distract myself from whatever thought was swirling around my head. I was a real joy to be around.

Eventually, I decided to get a doctor involved. I was a college student and poor, which meant I had really good health care: Medicaid. (Oddly enough, as a thirty-three-year-old working actor, I can't afford now what I could afford at the age of twenty-two. America yo!) I found a doctor and told her everything that was wrong with me. I'd never run down the entire list before, but as I heard myself, I could sense that dealing with this on my own was definitely no longer an option.

The doctor asked me if I wanted to kill myself.

I said, "Meh. Not yet, but when I do, I know how I'll do it."

I wasn't afraid to die, and if there was a button I could've pushed to erase my existence from Earth, I would've pushed it,

because it would've been easier and less messy than offing myself. According to the doctor, that was enough. She prescribed
an antidepressant and also suggested therapy. Dialectical behavioral therapy. I know, right? What's that?!

My doctor explained that dialectical behavioral therapy
(DBT) was a cognitive behavioral therapy designed to help
treat borderline personality disorder. I was eligible for a six-
month treatment program with group-therapy classes designed to help manage emotions and behaviors that could be
symptoms of borderline personality disorder. Classes were
Monday through Friday, from 12 p.m. to 3 p.m.

Did I have borderline personality disorder? Nope. Not at all.
But my doctor thought it was the best treatment my bomb-ass
insurance could buy for me. And because I was failing out of
college anyway, I had nothing but time. I was basically the perfect candidate for DBT even though my actual diagnosis was
only depression with a bit of an eating disorder. (I say "only"
and "a bit" like this wasn't absolutely ruining my life. I was going to die. LOL.) My doctor was really excited to get me into
the program. Possibly too excited, I remember thinking at the
time.

As my doctor described DBT and what it could do for me,
I sort of stopped listening. I nodded my head whenever she
paused; every now and then, I said, "Oh. Okay." But I couldn't
focus on anything back then. Not even someone talking directly to me in a quiet room. I was thinking about how I'd have
to drop out of school to do this therapy and whether or not it
would be worth it. I was thinking about how I'd tell my family.

I got home from the doctor's with a bottle full of antidepres-
sants and a new lease on life. I broke the news to my brother

first. I told Ahmed how I'd been feeling and how I had to get help for it. He suggested that I read the Bible and watch church on TV with him on Sunday mornings. He also told me he was sorry to know how badly I felt and that he wished he'd known, wished he could have helped. I should've told him sooner. I'd figured my brother was as self-centered as any twenty-some-thing guy. I didn't trust other people to care about me. In the case of Ahmed, I was wrong.

I chose to tell my mom while she was lying in bed asleep. I poked her until she was about half-awake, and then I pro-ceeded to relay the super important fact of my treatment for depression as though she were fully awake and able to receive the news. I was counting on her not being able to respond.

Look. My mom loves me more than I'll probably ever be able to comprehend. She wants the best life possible for me, and her fears for me come from love. With that in mind . . . my mom's first instinct was to tell me that what I was feeling I actually wasn't feeling — that I was just being dramatic. It felt like a slap in the face, but I realize now that she just wanted me not to feel like dying. She'd spent so much time trying to keep me alive that it broke her heart to imagine that I pre-ferred she hadn't. It hurt her to know I was hurting. She took it personally.

Her second instinct was to share a time in her life when she was upset and couldn't sleep. Just like me. She said that she just kept getting up and believing that God would pull her through and that He did. I was grateful that she opened up, but what she described was actually nothing like what I was going through. I couldn't make her understand that for me God wasn't enough. I couldn't make her understand that I couldn't get up on my own anymore.

So I started DBT: five days a week, three classes a day, each run by a different therapist. On two of those days I went to group therapy, and on Thursdays I went to one-on-one therapy. I was the youngest in the group by about ten years. A lot of the people in the group had gone through a few different cocktails of medication and therapy before DBT. Some had lived through suicide attempts and hospital stays in the psych ward. Some had spent years on a waiting list and had maxed out their savings to be able to attend the DBT classes. I, on the other hand, had basically waltzed in a day after mentioning my feelings to my doctor. I was on the lowest dosage of a bottom-shelf antidepressant, which was already working. And I was only twenty, so I had yet to ruin my life.

For me, the classes were fun! A lot of the program centered on keeping a diary and writing down my thoughts and feelings and then reading them aloud to everyone. I excelled at writing down my thoughts and feelings and reading them aloud to everyone! (Have you seen my Twitter?) I took to the program fast and was basically kicking my depression's ass. I was quickly becoming the Happiest Person at Sad Camp (that's literally what they called me).

This one woman hated me. She said that I was too perfect, that I was everyone's favorite, and that she was sick of it. She was a real bitch, but to be fair, she *was* suffering from borderline personality disorder. She was having a more difficult time than I was, and it must have been rough for her to see me smiling and laughing. Aside from her, most people in our class liked me. I made jokes about my pain and spent the first month of the program secretly feeling like I was mentally healthier than everyone else there and that I didn't need help as much as they did. (Oh, now I get why that bitch hated me.) Whether I was healthier or not, I *was* there with my DBT classmates because I *did,* in fact, need help. Most of my "happiness" was pretend and the jokes a cover-up. One of my therapists called it the "onion." He'd laugh at my inappropriate jokes, and then say, "Okay, Gabby, but peel the onion. What's under that joke? Hmm? Is it fear? Peel the onion." *Hippie.*

At first I'd think, *Shut up, Jacob! I saw you smoking a cigarette outside. You can't tell me shit!* But by the third month I was less judgmental. I was trying my best to be honest with everyone about my feelings, including myself. I was peeling the onion. I was also way more emotionally stable. I was still trying to shake the eating disorder, but I no longer wanted to die. I was grateful to the program and the doctor who had suggested it. The thoughts I'd had, the absence of any fear of death, the uncontrollable emotional sadness . . . I didn't know anymore who the fuck that girl was, but she was no longer me. And she's definitely not the person writing this today.

One thing didn't change, though: I was still hooking up with random dudes. It took a while longer to learn that I deserved to at least like someone before letting him rub up against me. In time I started to believe I was worth more than being fucked and forgotten. I decided to try celibacy for a while. Except I wasn't going to be a weirdo about it and tell everyone.

"You'd better really fight. It would be so hard on you because you're still a virgin, and that's not how you want to lose your virginity," my mother repeated. This is how much she believed her own statement: she said it twice. She peered at me, waiting for a response.

I suddenly realized, in the midst of my stunned silence, that my mom thought we were a lot closer than we actually were. She thought that since telling her about my depression had been such a success I would have told her about losing my virginity when it happened. She thought I was a delicate little flower. And she thought I was a little bit sad for being twenty-seven and *still* a virgin.

How could I tell her?

"True, I'll fight like hell, Mom. Could you make me a sandwich?"

3

WHY YOU SHOULDN'T MARRY FOR A GREEN CARD

The story of two people who got married,
met and then fell in love.

— tagline from the movie *Green Card*

THERE ARE LOTS OF WAYS I could describe my mom, Alice Tan Ridley. Free-spirited hippie is one (actually, I'm the only one who calls her a hippie, and never have I done it to her face). She doesn't care about rules and breaks them often. She wants other people to live their lives the way they want to. She wishes it was socially acceptable for straight men to cry and wear dresses and skirts. (That being said, she told me to have her buried in pants.)

My mom is everyone's favorite aunt. She was the youngest girl of nine kids, all born and raised on a dirt road in a town you've never heard of in Georgia. She has a ton of sisters who had children when she was a little girl, so she's been helping raise kids all her life. She became an assistant preschool teacher at the age of thirteen. Really, she's been trained in the art of fun since birth.

She's comfortable in her own skin and knows how gorgeous she is. If you happen to think she's not gorgeous, you're wrong. She's the most confident person in the room. Any room. She's the most talented person around for miles. Perhaps for a thousand miles. Definitely in the city. She shines as bright as a diamond because she is a goddamned STAR! That's another phrase I use to describe my mother—again, never to her face.

Whether what I've said about my mom is objectively true or not, it's the way she feels about herself, and so, in a very "I think, therefore I am" way, it becomes true because it's *her* truth. That kind of confidence is rare. I've been trying to feel that special brand of confidence all my life, but I still fall short of it. Don't get me wrong, I'm great! But Mom's confidence is incredible and hypnotic, like a magic show. Can you imagine being her daughter? It's annoying. Like a magic show.

When Ahmed and I came along, my mom worked in the New York City Public Schools as a paraprofessional, teaching in a class of differently abled children. Her students had Down syndrome, cerebral palsy, and other disabilities. Whenever her class went on a trip to the zoo or the circus or even to see a WWF match at Madison Square Garden, she'd take us along, too. When I started going to school, it was to the same one where my mom taught. At least once a day I'd ask for the bathroom pass, and I'd go visit her in her classroom, grab a snack, say what up to my homies, and then go back to my own classroom.

Alice has worked as a professional singer since childhood,

and even while she was teaching, she had her own show: a gospel brunch every Sunday at the famed Cotton Club in Harlem. She was always singing. She would sing the national anthem at school assemblies and perform in choirs at different churches, but her Cotton Club show was an actual job. She had an amazing voice that she certainly didn't intend to waste.

Entertaining came naturally. On the bus or train, my mom would play I Spy with my brother and me or tell us the story "Sleeping Ugly," a tale she made up about a girl so ugly she fell asleep waiting for a prince to marry her. A lot of times, my mom would spin a fairy tale out of whatever she'd watched on TV after my brother and I had gone to bed. Other passengers would listen in on our stories and laugh along with us. I hated them, because I hate strangers. My mom, on the other hand, smiled right back at them. There was always enough happiness to go around with my mom.

That's why her marriage to my dad made no sense to me as a child.

My dad has always seemed to me the most boring man in the world. He doesn't laugh, and he smiles less than he laughs. He is a cabdriver. I've always thought of that as being as much a description of his personality as his occupation. I remember him being at work all the time. Sometimes he'd drive us to school in the morning, but most times he didn't. He seemed to hate the sound of his children's laughter. Sometimes while he was out, my brother and I would be in my parents' bed with my mom. She'd tickle us and give us rides on her back while she tried to knock us off. We'd be giggling away, and then we'd hear the front door slam, and my mom would say, "Uh-oh. Mr. Man is here."

That door slam meant the fun was officially over. Suddenly, my dad would appear in the doorway of the bedroom with his nose turned up. "Giggle, giggle, giggle! All you do is giggle! All the time laughing, God dammy! So loud! I can hear you from the elevator!" Then he'd go to the kitchen to have dinner. By himself. My mom would roll her eyes and quietly imitate him, and I'd laugh again. Loudly. And that's not a typo, by the way. "God dammy" is the way my dad pronounces the phrase *goddamn it*. He's African, so he has an accent. *African* is another word I use to describe his personality. African, cab-driver, boring.

My dad wanted us to live in constant fear of him because he saw fear as a sign of respect. But since I didn't really fear him, I constantly got in trouble for being disrespectful. In part, this was because of my laugh. My laugh has always sounded more like a shrill scream followed by a loud snort than a proper laugh. If people could choose what their laughs sound like, I'd probably go with something that didn't sound like it lived under a bridge and gave fairy-tale characters the business on their way to Grandmother's house. My dad hated my laugh and always thought I could change it—that I just wasn't trying hard enough. He would threaten to glue my lips shut so he wouldn't have to hear it. Other times he'd threaten to glue my mouth *and* my butt shut so when I laughed or farted I would explode. That's really what he said! I know it sounds horrifying, but it's the funniest thing he's ever said. (He was best at being unintentionally funny.) I'd pretend to be afraid of him, but as soon as I was alone, I'd laugh my glued-up ass off.

When I was around six years old, my father and I had a big argument. It started when he mentioned his plan to live with me in his old age. He said that I'd have to take care of him, and cook and clean for him like a good Muslim woman, and on and on—

Oh, yeah! I was born Muslim. But the year before this conversation, when I was five, I made the conscious decision to stop being one. I'll be honest: I wanted to eat bacon like my mom and had already had warnings about that cooking and cleaning bullshit, so the choice was easy.

Now it was time to tell my dad there was no way I was letting him live with me and my future husband and kids. I didn't even like living with him *then*. To summarize my side of the fight, I said something to the effect of "Hell NO!"

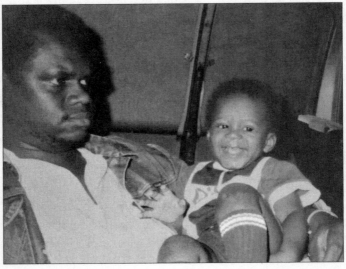

Courtesy of Gabourey Sidibe

Dad and Ahmed This is one of my favorite photos of Ahmed as a baby. I wasn't born yet so he's actually pretty happy. I'm the worst thing that's ever happened to that kid. My dad looks like he's trying really hard not to smile. Dork.

"When you were a baby," he answered, "you'd sleep right here on my chest! On this chest! You loved it so much!" He was trying to guilt his way into my future home.

"That was years ago!" I yelled back. "My husband and I will be too busy for you to live with us! I can't afford it!"

In the end, my dad resolved to have more children who would love him more than I did and who would be grateful to have him live with them. I wished him luck then, and I wish him luck now. More than twenty-five years later I still don't want to live with my dad.

The point is, my mom and dad were like night and day. When my dad was at work, the house was filled with laughter; and when my mom was gone, the house was dark and either too cold or too hot. Uncomfortable. I always thought that Bill Withers's song "Ain't No Sunshine When She's Gone" was about my mother. So how could these two very different people have come together to find enough love to get married and have kids?

The American Dream!

My father, Ibnou Sidibe, is from Senegal. His father was a politician who served as mayor of the third largest city in Senegal, Thiès (pronounced *chess*). Dad was his second son from his second marriage. The oldest son died at two years, leaving my father as the oldest boy, a very important position in a Senegalese family. Dad was sent to school in France to be an architect. Sometime after graduating, he figured he'd move to America. I've never asked him why—I always assumed it was to make his fortune, like in some fairy tale with him selling his prized cow for magic beans to grow a beanstalk to make a boat to sail to America. There is no evidence that my dad sailed here in a boat made out of a beanstalk that grew from magic beans that were purchased after the sale of an exceptional cow, but I've always preferred that idea. My dad has always been so boring that wherever there's a blank space in his life story I fill it with whimsy in an attempt to like him more.

In all probability, he took a plane over. He stayed with family members or friends of family or wherever he could. He even slept in the hallways of hotels and apartment buildings, but I don't think he did that for too long. He learned English pretty quickly, made friends, got a room, and found a few jobs. In order to stay in this country, though, he needed to find a wife. He let his new friends know of his plan, and through them, Ibnou met Alice. He offered her about $4,000 to marry him so he could get his green card.

She agreed. My mom says that she cared about him as a person and that that's why she married him. She says the money wasn't important.

My father courted her for a whole year after they got married before she finally fell for him enough to sleep with him. That's right! My mom is so classy that you have to marry her and *then* wait a year before she gives you any play. He took her to Africa to his hometown, and that's when she says she actually fell in love with him and decided that he was her husband for real and that they'd build a life together.

Before she visited Africa, she thought it was filled with savages with spears in their hands chasing lions. My mom grew up a dark-skinned girl in the most racist part of America: the Deep South. She survived "Whites Only" drinking fountains and the KKK knocking on her door looking for an uncle. Hollywood—Hollywood, where shiny tan white people play

Egyptian pharaohs and queens—never told my mom that Cleopatra looked like her. That Cleopatra had dark skin and a round body. But when my mom landed in Senegal, she saw a sea of black people who looked like her. Who looked like her mother and father, like her entire family. And they were beautiful. They were doctors, lawyers, artists, mothers, sisters, brothers, fathers. None of them were savages. None of them were powerless people stolen and enslaved to build a nation that would kill and condemn them. Africa was a mirror to my mother. It was home. It's easy to fall in love with Africa. It's easy to fall in love *in* Africa. I believe that my mother fell in love with Africa, *not* with Ibnou. (That's my theory, anyway.) Why else would my mom ignore the two major signs of impending doom that accompanied her green-card-but-I-care-for-you marriage?

Sign one: My mother and my father's mother looked like twins. Really! Everyone in my dad's family looks just like everyone in my mom's family. Even my dad is identical to my mother's brother, and not in a general "they all look alike" way. As it turns out, my mother's ancestors, who were stolen from Africa and sold into slavery, were taken from Senegal. A blood test confirmed that Alice's ancestors are Ibnou's ancestors. My mother and father have the same bloodline! Isn't that gross? Furthermore, they were both carriers of the same genetic blood disorder, hemoglobin C disease, which causes an abnormal breakdown of the red blood cells. They were told to not have children together. That was *before* they fell in love! *Before* Africa! After Africa, my mother apparently forgot all about the downside of marrying someone whose mother looked just like her.

Sign two: My dad's ex-girlfriend. Yes! While they were in my dad's hometown, my father introduced my mother to his first cousin Tola. He had dated Tola before he left Senegal for school in France. Upon meeting Alice, Tola asked if she could be my mother's wife-in-law. You see, men in Senegal are allowed to marry multiple women at one time. Polygamy. My grandfather had more than one wife and many children. The wives all lived in separate homes with their children, and my grandfather sort of moved around from home to home, family to family. It's their culture. This is the life my father was raised to lead, and the life that my grandmother and most Senegalese women were raised to accept.

Not Alice, though. She let Ibnou know that if he wanted to marry Tola he'd have to divorce her first. Ibnou assured Alice that it was all over between him and Tola, and that he was dedicated to Alice and their new marriage. She believed him. After leaving Africa, Alice took Ibnou to Georgia to meet her family before they went back home to New York City. A year later, they had Ahmed, who was born with hemoglobin C disease. Barely three months after giving birth to my brother, my mother became pregnant with me. There was a three-in-four chance that I would be born with the same blood disorder, but as would become the theme of my life, I beat the odds. Less than three years into their green-card-but-I-care-for-you marriage, Alice and Ibnou had the perfect nuclear family in a three-bedroom apartment with a terrace in one of Brooklyn's roughest neighborhoods: Bed-Stuy (birthplace of Notorious B.I.G., Jay Z, and me!). And they lived happily ever after. Oh, wait! Not really!

I can't remember a time when I didn't know that my parents

were unhappily married. It wasn't that they always fought. They did, but it was more than that. The three of us—my mom, Ahmed, and I—seemed to live an entirely different life than my father. He was either gone at work or reading the paper in silence. He was impenetrable. I remember calling his name for minutes, a foot away from him, and him just ignoring me. We weren't on his radar unless we were being yelled at or made fun of. I was "Fatso" and Ahmed was "Freeda," a girl's name that Ibnou called him when he thought my brother was acting like a sissy. When I argued with Ibnou, he hit me, and I cried, and he felt guilty and called me his princess. Sometimes he gave me money. I figured out very early on that he was always nice when I made him feel bad, so I started to cry on cue (this skill came in handy when I became an actor). He often hit us to make the point that we belonged to him, that we were his property, and that he could do with us what he wanted. This was never okay with Alice, and she fussed at him and fought with him to protect us. So he started to hit us only when she wasn't around.

I took to speaking in a baby voice in a misguided attempt to appear cuter so I'd be in less trouble. (I was a creep then; I'm a creep now.) My father would say stuff to my mom like "We need to have another baby. She would grow up if we had another baby, and she'd stop talking like that." My mom would always respond, "I will NEVER have another child with you ever again! You mistreat the kids you have. I'm not having more so you can mistreat them, too." See? I knew they were unhappily married. I hoped that my mom would leave Ibnou eventually. I couldn't wait!

To be clear, I don't think my dad was intentionally abusive.

He was trying to make us better children and therefore better people. More to the point, he was trying to make us into the kind of children he could recognize: quiet children who listened to him without question. He wanted children who were like him, so he raised us the way his father raised *him*. Ahmed and I were too foreign; we had too much personality.

My father went back home to Senegal frequently. He'd usually take Ahmed and me with him, but once, when I was around four and Ahmed was five, he and Ahmed went alone. They were gone for more than a month. When they came back, Ahmed told my mom and me about a party our dad had taken him to. It was at a big house, and there were a lot of people there, and they kept giving Dad money. I was pissed I'd missed such a great party with free money, but now I know

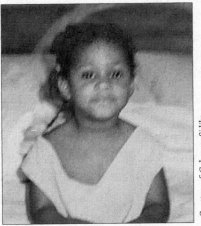

Courtesy of Gabourey Sidibe

Baby Gabou My parents would send Ahmed and me to Mom's parents' house in Georgia during the summer. I wish I could remember those times, but I was too little. I mean, look at that little nose of mine! Can you even, cuz I can't. I CAN'T EVEN!

better: we were listening to my brother describe my dad's wedding. Yes. Ibnou had gone to Senegal to marry Tola as he'd always promised her he would (and as he always promised my mom he wouldn't). I'm certain that if Ibnou had taken me instead of Ahmed I would've come home and yelled, "Mommy! Daddy married this other lady!" Ahmed was far more innocent; he believed in goodness and hope or whatever. I was born a cynical, suspicious, forty-five-year-old divorcée. I would've reported every single thing that I saw at that wedding, and the jig would've been up as soon as I was back in America.

But the fact is, Ahmed was there—not me—so for the time being, nothing much changed. Until two years later, when my mom was out of town on a trip, and my dad came home to our apartment with a baby.

"This is your brother Malick," he said to us.

The baby was about a year old. Dad handed him to me.

"You're not a baby anymore," he very clearly said to me. "You can't talk like a baby anymore. This is a baby. You're a big girl now. No more, okay!?"

"Yes, Daddy," I said, sounding more like a baby than I ever had. (I would decide when the game was over, not him.)

I loved the shit out of that baby, but I didn't believe he was my brother. Africans are always calling strangers their sisters, brothers, mothers, fathers, aunts, and uncles. It doesn't mean that you're actually related.

"Where'd this baby come from?" I asked.

"The airport," Ibnou answered.

"Where was he before the airport? Who made this baby?"

"I did," he answered.

"For real? You made this baby? With who? Are we keeping this baby forever? Where's this baby gonna sleep? Who's gonna teach this baby English? Does Mommy know this baby? Can we afford this baby?"

Ibnou recanted. "This is just your cousin. This is my brother's baby. He's just visiting! He's going back tonight! This is not my baby. You are just like your mammy!" He was always telling me that I was like my mom. He pronounced it *mammy*. Adorable.

I stopped asking questions and went back to trying to force that baby to love me. Later that night, Ibnou took the baby back to the airport to go home with Tola. I didn't meet her. Yet.

When Alice came home from her trip, I yelled, "Mommy! Daddy brought a baby here! He said it's my brother! Daddy has a baby!" She assumed the same thing I assumed: Africans are always claiming everyone's family when they really aren't.

Two years later, Tola came to live with us. All I knew was that she was Dad's cousin and the mother of baby Malick who'd come to America for a day. But this time she came alone and Malick stayed in Africa. How did it happen that Tola came to live with us? Well, Ibnou had convinced Alice to write a letter to Tola inviting her. By this point, Ibnou had been granted U.S. citizenship, but because Tola wasn't an American citizen, a natural-born American (Alice) had to issue the invitation. Ibnou had convinced Alice to help a sister of his come to America the same way, so this was nothing new and didn't seem suspicious. It may seem suspicious to you because you're hearing the story all at once. In real time, though, Ibnou's con took years to pull off.

So Tola was finally in America, and like when Ibnou's sister came to America and stayed with us (another story for another time), I had to share my room and my bed. This was awful for me because I was, and still am, a solitary creature. I hate strangers, as I've said, and I hate houseguests. Ibnou once told me that every time anyone came over to our house, I'd incessantly ask when that person was leaving. I believe it. Even now, whenever a friend comes over to my apartment, I count down the minutes until they're gone so I can finally take my pants off. (Adulthood is all about waiting to take your pants off.)

Anyway, Tola stayed with us for three or four months. Alice was super welcoming and even took Tola to buy her first winter coat. Tola cooked and cleaned, but in my opinion she wasn't particularly interesting. She was just another boring African in our house I couldn't wait to get rid of. She was another Ibnou.

Ibnou eventually found his cousin/secret wife an apartment about a ten-minute walk away from ours. That's when he stopped coming home at night. One morning, on the way to school, Alice went over to Tola's new apartment unannounced. Ibnou was there, and Alice saw his clothes on the side of Tola's bed. He swore that he was just talking to her and then got too tired to come home so he slept there — that they were just sleeping, that's all. Alice said okay and left.

At this point you're probably thinking, *Girl! Just leave him!!* That's what I'm thinking while writing this. That's what I *was* thinking — and most likely saying — back then, too.

But that's because there are things that I didn't consider. Like the fact that two years before, when Ahmed was seven

and I was six, Ibnou and Alice got into an argument, and in order to punish her, he called the Bureau of Child Welfare and
accused her of abusing Ahmed and me.

It was a nice, normal afternoon until the Bureau of Child Welfare picked us up. I was looking forward to coming home from
school because I knew we had orange ice cream in the fridge
and Chips Ahoy! in the cupboard. I wanted to get a bowl of
that ice cream and stick two cookies on top and watch cartoons. This was *all* I could think about, and even now it's the
strongest memory I have of that day. What I didn't know was
that BCW had stopped by our school earlier in the day. Because my mother taught there and was in the building, she'd
been able to cut them off before they pulled us from class;
she begged them to pick us up from home instead so that our
classmates wouldn't see.

I'd just put the ice cream back in the freezer when two
agents knocked on the door. Ahmed and I were taken by a
black woman with curly hair and another person whose face
I can't pull from my memory. He must've been white and
male. Ahmed and I were separated and taken to different foster homes. He went to a big family somewhere in Queens with
parents who were nice to him (they took him to IHOP). I went
to more of an *Annie* kind of foster home run by a pair of identical twin sisters. They were identically mean and each had a
son the same age as I was. There were two other boys there
and one teenage girl who refused to talk to anyone. The twins
threatened to spank us if we didn't do what they said. And
even though they fed their biological kids hot meals every day
and night, the foster kids got only peanut butter and jelly sand-

wiches. That's true abuse. The twins cut my hair and put ribbons in it for picture day at the new school they enrolled me in.

It was awful. To this day, I don't know if I was in Brooklyn or Queens. I didn't know my way home. I didn't know what I'd said to end up there. I didn't know where my brother was, or if I'd see him or any of my family ever again.

Alice was blindsided. Of course she wasn't abusing either of us. Ibnou had only said that to hurt her. When he called BCW, he imagined they'd remove *Alice,* that he'd be punishing *her.* He didn't expect them to take me and Ahmed. In order to get us back, both Ibnou and Alice had to endure an investigation. Alice left work every day and went straight to the courthouse with every scrap of documentation she could think of that would help to get us back. After we were in foster care for almost three weeks, BCW agents took us home, and only then did we learn what had happened, that *Dad had done this to us.* After that, I was finished. I was officially over him, and I started my campaign for Mom to get a divorce. But Alice was biding her time. She wanted out of that marriage, but she knew she had to do it in a way that would keep Ahmed and me safe. It was around this time that Alice started giving Ahmed and me safety drills. She told us to kick and scream if Ibnou or a friend of his ever tried to pick us up from school when she hadn't discussed it with us first. She told us to kick and scream if we were ever with Ibnou and he drove us to the airport without her knowing it. The eighties were so crazy, y'all!

Now fast-forward a couple of years: Ibnou is asking Alice to write a letter to Tola inviting her to America, and Alice is finally seeing her opportunity approaching.

• • •

The summer after Tola joined us in America, Alice and her Cotton Club band were asked to perform at a festival in Morocco. She wanted to go but knew my dad couldn't take care of us on his own as he had to work and Ahmed and I were too young to stay by ourselves. So it was decided that Tola would move back into our apartment to take care of us while my mom was gone. There I was, back to sharing my bed with a fully grown woman.

The night before my mother was scheduled to come home, Ahmed and I did something we used to do a lot back then: we woke up in the middle of the night and met each other in the hallway to discuss the dreams we'd been having or whether or not cartoons were on TV. But that night, the night before Mom came home, I had something else to discuss.

"Tola's not in my bed," I said.

"Have you seen her?"

"No. She's not in the living room, either."

I looked past Ahmed to our parents' room. The door was closed. I knew then that Tola and my father were sleeping together. It was the first time the thought had ever entered my head, but I knew I was right. I knew that Ibnou was super boring and straight up the *worst,* but the idea that he would cheat on my mom with someone he introduced to us as his cousin had never occurred to me. That was some soap opera shit that didn't happen to real people. Ahmed, still innocent, had no idea what was going on. It's not that he's dumb; he's just sweet and more willing to let people live their lives. He's like Mom that way. Me? I'm like Ibnou — suspicious of everyone and personally offended by everything.

When Alice came home the next day, I was so happy to have

her back that I decided to enjoy the moment and wait on reporting Tola's disappearance from my room. I didn't have to wait long. Tola spent the night (again) in my bed (again); after all the celebrating, it was too late for her to go home (I guess). Alice and Ibnou made love (or whatever, GROSS), and they both went to the bathroom afterward to take a shower together (Eeewwwww! Just more GROSS!). Tola walked in on them and had a breakdown. She started crying and yelling at Ibnou in Wolof. Then she ran out of the house. Ibnou explained to Alice that Tola was just shocked. Married people having sex? Weird and gross! I get it, Tola!

Alice knew what was going on and took advantage of the moment to force the truth. She went after Tola and cornered her in a hallway.

"Tola, are you sleeping with Ibnou?"

"No, no! He's just my cousin," she lied.

"Is he your husband?" Alice pressed on.

"No! No! He's my cousin! That's it!"

Alice thought for a second, and asked about Tola's baby, Malick, left behind in Africa.

"Is Malick Ibnou's bastard son?"

If you know Muslims, the word *bastard* is a strong trigger. My entire life, my father told me never to bring home any bastards, that pregnancy out of wedlock was a sin worse than most, and that the shame it would bring would be irreversible and I could never bring him that shame. Calling Tola's son a bastard was a knife to her pride and dignity.

"NO! He's not a bastard! We're married!" Tola answered.

Finally. After years of being secretly married to his cousin, fathering her child, and bringing his second wife into the home of his first wife, Ibnou was caught red-handed. He had lied and schemed for as long as he possibly could, but now the truth was out, and he had no choice but to let Alice walk away with me and Ahmed.

The next day Alice took Ahmed and me shopping for new clothes for the beginning of the school year. I was going into fourth grade. She told us that we were moving out, finally leaving Ibnou and finally getting out of Brooklyn. We packed, and Ibnou didn't protest at all. What we didn't know then was that Tola was pregnant again—that Ibnou had a new family coming in right after us. We moved into a bedroom in my aunt Dorothy's brownstone in Harlem. Three months later Tola gave birth to another son, and they eventually brought Malick to America along with an older daughter of Tola's from a pre-

Courtesy of Gabourey Sidibe

Family Portrait LASERS!!! Weren't the '80s the best? Also, how perfect is my mom's roller set?! And her eyebrows are arched all to be damned! Get into this BLACK QUEEN!

vious relationship. The five of them were a seemingly happy family. I can't super tell as all of them were always just sitting around silently watching French news. Eventually, Ibnou married Tola here in America so that she could get her own green card.

Ibnou and Alice remained friends no matter what I had to say about it. He'd mistreated us all, hit us whenever he wanted, sent us to foster care, secretly married his cousin, brought her into our home, had a family with her behind our backs, and forced us to move to Harlem into a single bedroom with two twin beds while his new family took our place. Alice's power to forgive astounded me. She still welcomed my dad into our home, and my dad was always around. He didn't pay child support because, in addition to Tola, he went on to marry other women in Africa and have child after child.

Today Ibnou is in his sixties and still having kids. He has more children than we know of. He's far from the guy who once threatened to glue my lips shut if I laughed too loud, and I'm not the little girl who could see only African, cabdriver, and boring in him. But our relationship is . . . complicated. I'm still trying to look at my relationship with Ibnou the way Alice does. She always says, "Don't let anyone else take away your joy. If they don't want to be with you or around you, let them go. Pick up your shit and keep going. You came into the world by yourself, and the next person's lungs don't help you breathe."

She's so smart. Even if she did marry someone whose mother looked *exactly* like her.

4

A PSYCHIC TOLD ME SO

*Gabby, you're a little bit psychic and
a lotta bit psycho.*

— Jussie Smollett

OH! I TOTALLY FORGOT to tell you that Tola was a psychic! At least that's how she made her living. When Mom, Ahmed, and I moved out of our Brooklyn apartment and Tola moved in with Dad, Ahmed's old room became her office. When I say *office,* I'm being generous. It was still mostly Ahmed's bedroom, with his bed still in it. Tola would have her clients come into his room, and she'd sit on the floor while they sat on the bed or across from her on the floor. She had a satchel of cowry shells, and she apparently was able to read them in order to tell the future. When I was a kid, I believed this without question. I thought we all did, so I never bothered asking if she really was psychic or not. I didn't think people could fake something like that. Aww! I was so young and innocent!

In the early days after they broke up, my parents made an attempt at shared custody. Ahmed and I would go back to Brooklyn on Friday after school and return to our aunt Dorothy's house in Harlem on Monday after school. All weekend long, I'd be in our old apartment with its new furniture, new smells, new stepmother, new baby brother. The apartment I'd grown up in didn't seem familiar without Mom in it. Without my family in it. There were a few pictures on a shelf of Ahmed and me, but they seemed out of place. We looked like two American children in the home of an African family. Dad and Tola spoke to each other in Wolof. I knew only a little Wolof from visiting Senegal and could not really understand what they were talking about. The only American voices around were mine and Ahmed's, and neither seemed to count. We were the foreigners now. When Tola had her second son, my brother Abdul, teaching me to be a "good Muslim woman and mother" started being important again for Dad. So I had to help Tola with the newborn while Dad was driving a cab around New York City. That was fine by me. I loved Abdul and didn't want to miss a second of watching him be a baby. Even though I was by then only nine years old, it was my job to tend to Abdul while Tola had customers.

Africans from lots of different countries came to see Tola for insight into their futures. People from Senegal like her and Dad, people from Mali, Nigeria, South Africa, everywhere! For me, it was like a rainbow of all different shades and cultures of black and brown. Once while I was there, Af-

rican Americans came! It was a Sunday. I remember because
the two older black women had come straight from church
dressed to the nines in church clothes. One wore all yellow
with a white hat. The other woman wore all white with a
black-and-white hat. I loved them. I was so excited to see another American in that apartment. It was as if I'd been lost in
another country where I didn't speak the language but then
turned a corner and saw a McDonald's and knew I'd be okay.
When the church ladies arrived, Tola was with another customer so they sat in the living room with me while I watched
The Kids in the Hall on Comedy Central and overfed Abdul.
I was usually pretty quiet with the Africans who came for a
reading. I liked speaking to them just enough to hear their accents and dialects, but then I usually returned to whatever TV
show I was watching at the time, so conversation was mini-
mal. Not on African American Day! I asked those ladies intrusive question after intrusive question. I asked why they
wanted a reading, how they'd heard of Tola, and where their
church was. They asked if Abdul was my child or my brother.
Rude. They commented that my English was really good. I
thanked them and told them that I had been practicing since
I was around a year old. They seemed impressed but only because they didn't realize I was being sarcastic. I loved those
black ladies. Not only did they remind me of Mom and what
our apartment used to feel like, but they helped me realize
that Tola could be a psychic for all kinds of people. Somehow
I had assumed she could only do readings for African people
—that she was talking to African spirits who told her the secret futures of other African people. Remember, I was nine

years old. But now it occurred to me that if she could do a reading for these black ladies maybe she could tell me what my future would be too!

One summer night after I had turned ten, I asked her to tell me my future. She laughed like I was cute and said yes. She got her cowry shells, and we sat on the floor in the living room while Dad watched French news on TV. (I swear to God he is always watching French news. He must really worry about what goes on there.) By now, Abdul was walking, but I was holding him hostage in my lap because I couldn't feel him loving me if he wasn't in my arms. Tola asked me what I wanted to know. What I really wanted to know was if I was ever going to have a boyfriend. I wanted to know if Thomas who lived in the building had a crush on me the way I had a crush on him. I wanted to know if I was going to get my period soon. But Dad was five feet away on the couch, so those questions seemed inappropriate to ask. Instead, I giggled and rolled my eyes. "I don't know! The future! I just want to know . . . like the future and stuff." She picked up her shells and shook them in her hand a few times and then dropped a few in a bowl she'd placed on the floor between us. She picked those shells up again, shook them again, and threw them into the bowl once more.

"I see a big future for you," she finally said.

"Am I gonna be a therapist!?" I excitedly asked.

Tola didn't understand what I had asked so she ignored it, and said, "You gonna be famous."

Whoa! I didn't see that coming at all. Sure, I had wanted to be a comedian when I was a little younger, but I'd given up on that dream when I was eight. I'd also never envisioned being famous that way. I had mostly wanted to be a comedian so I could go to nightclubs and travel.

"As a girl comic?" I asked.

Again, Tola didn't understand my question, but she said, "No. I don't know. But famous, yes!"

"How?" I asked.

"I don't know, but you gonna be famous," she reassured me.

This wasn't adding up. By now, Mom was no longer a paraprofessional schoolteacher and was instead a prominent subway performer. (Hold on, I'll tell you about this a little later.) She was making lots of fans down there, and Ahmed and I were sure that one day she'd be discovered, and then she'd be famous and on the radio, and we'd be rich, and Dad and his new stupid family, Tola included, would be sorry for making us move away and turning our old apartment into Little Senegal, and then Mom would adopt Abdul. Then we'd be happy. That was the plan. I thought that's what Tola would see. I wasn't sure how she'd come up with *me* being famous.

"Are you sure?"

She picked up the shells, shook them, and threw them in the bowl again.

"Yes. You gonna be famous like Oprah."

"Are you sure you don't mean my *mom's* gonna be famous?" Tola looked down at the shells without picking them up again. She looked like she was really seeing something in those shells. Like she was watching something that she didn't completely understand.

"Your mom . . . little bit. *You. You* are famous. Your mom is famous because you are famous." Well, shit. I wasn't sure why she saw me being more famous, but it seemed great to me! Great *and* suspicious.

"What else?" I asked, eager for more.

"You get skinny." Now this was really starting to sound good.

"Word! Dad! I'm gonna get skinny!" I excitedly shared the news with him. He laughed one of his rare laughs.

"You gonna have twins when you grow up," Tola said. "Two babies. Girl."

Now she was getting out of hand. I let Abdul crawl out of my lap far away from me and my womb. I mean . . . it was possible. My maternal grandmother was a twin, I knew, so maybe they ran in my family. But twins sounded expensive. One baby was fun, but I didn't know how I would afford two whole babies at one time.

"Will I be rich?" I asked.

"*Mmhmm,*" she answered.

"Oh, good. That's good." Stupid question. I was going to be famous. Of course I'd be rich, too! Duh! If Tola knew I'd be famous and rich, then clearly she was the greatest psychic in the world. *And* I was about to be skinny, too? No wonder every African in the city traveled to Bed-Stuy to see her. Bitch was spitting out straight facts!

"So, I'm gonna have a husband?" I asked. As if Dad would ever allow me to have kids out of wedlock.

"Of course," Tola answered. "Your husband is a good Muslim man." My face fell. If looks could kill, Tola would've been long gone. As an adult, I've known many great dudes who happen to be Muslim. But when I was a child, marrying a Muslim meant marrying my father. That was something I knew by the age of five I wasn't going to do.

"You're gonna be a good Muslim wife to a good African Muslim man," Tola continued. That's when I realized that she wasn't really psychic. She couldn't have been. I wasn't capable of being a "good Muslim wife" any more than Mom was able to be when she was married to Dad.

I told Mom about my reading, and we laughed about it together. Twins? Fame? Me, a "good Muslim wife"? I figured that being able to laugh about it afterward was probably why people went to psychics anyway. Three years later, Tola gave birth to twins. Two girls. That was all the confirmation I needed: Tola *might* be psychic, but her sight wasn't straight.

I maybe believe in psychics. I admit that. I believe some people have the ability to sense things in a clearer way than most. I believe that we all have a sense of intuition but some of us have an innate capacity to see something that has yet to happen. If that ability is so strong that you can actually charge people for it, I'm cool. Mom says that her mother was psychic. That if MaDear (that's what my family calls my grandmother, ya know, like those Tyler Perry movies) said something would happen, it always did. Mom also says that when she was a little girl she found herself to be psychic as well. She said she would dream about a family in Africa that was just like hers in Georgia and that the dream felt like a memory, not a dream. But this scared her, so she prayed for God to take the power away from her and, according to Mom, He did. I just called Mom a few minutes ago to confirm all of this, and she says she doesn't remember asking for God to take the power away. And that she would never say that she or her mother was psychic for sure. I still believe we are an intuitive family but that this intuition is just part of being a woman. Women get to give birth, and they get to know you're going to screw up your life if you get a neck tattoo. Maybe being psychic runs in my family. More likely, thinking that you're much more special and talented than anyone else runs in my family.

Along the same suspicious lines, Tola very well could've told me what she thought I wanted to hear. I was a kid, after all. If she could really read those shells, why didn't they tell her how much I hated her and Dad? Where were those shells when I had to share my room and bed with Dad's mistress who was pretending to be just his cousin? Was it the shells that told Tola I was unhappy and suffering in that apartment with them? She more likely had some compassion for me and decided to tell me that I'd be rich and famous so that I'd feel better. (I am not saying this was a terrible thing, but it doesn't make Tola psychic.) If she was really psychic, she should've told me to wear underwear on the day in seventh grade when I broke my ankle and had to get a cast put on my foot while trying to cover my vag with a notebook. Thanks *a lot,* Tola! The fact that she eventually was proven right about my being famous means nothing. It could just be a coincidence.

5

#BLACKGIRLMAGIC

Gabby SidiBae

@GabbySidibe

I need to make friends with a cool girl in my building who wouldn't mind coming over to help me take my weave out. #goals

6:44 PM - Mar 21 2015

THINK I LIKE THE IDEA of psychics because I'm often bored with day-to-day things. It's more fun to fantasize about what *will* or *should* happen. My life is way better in my head. I can do anything up there. For instance, I have a recurring and very real fantasy about shaving my head. In my fantasy, I'm standing in a beautifully lit bedroom with French windows. I'm wearing pink silk pajamas, like what TLC wore in the "Creep" video. I'm staring into the distance. Flower petals are floating onto my face, and a soft wind is caressing my pj's. An electric razor floats through the room into my hands. I slowly buzz away my hair, line by line, until it's all gone. Then I smile. I'm finally happy.

I'm always working on a movie or TV show, which means that most of the year what I look like is in the hands of more people than I can count. If I want to cut my hair, I can't do it without discussing it first with four producers, a show runner, and the head of the hair department. I have to ask permission, and then there has to be a meeting. I spend seven months of every year wearing a blonde wig while filming each season of the show *Empire*. It's exactly like when I was fourteen and Mom said I couldn't get a nose ring. Except *Empire* pays me more than Mom, so I'm more inclined to do what they say. (I still slam my bedroom door and silently mutter, "I hate it here!" under my breath.)

But I'm on vacation now, so my hair is my own again! Right now it's in long extensions that are twisted into braids. It's called a Senegalese twist. The twists are a medium brown with supposedly honey brown highlights. Ya know what? The highlights are actually just straight-up *blonde,* and I need to admit that to myself. This is not the color I wanted. I wanted black hair to match my own natural color. I wanted something subtle, because I'm not the kind of person who takes risks with my appearance. My whole life has been a struggle to blend in, and colored hair feels like drawing a target around my face. So how did I end up blonde?

When I went down to Thirty-fourth Street to the weave store to buy my hair (Yes! I go to the store to buy hair. Don't pretend you haven't seen *Good Hair*), the fast-talking saleswoman suggested I go with lighter colors. She seemed much more confident than I felt, and I was feeling less confident and increasingly uncomfortable by the minute because people were starting to notice me. This wasn't a great hair day for me. The night before I'd cut out my weave, so I was in the hair shop wearing a wig, a black Yankees cap, and sunglasses. I'd meant to be sort of incognito, but one of the salesclerks had already asked if I'd take a picture with the employees, and a customer had asked if I was "the famous Gabrielle Swordbee." I wanted to get the hell out of there. I was too uncomfortable to think clearly about highlights, so I just said yes to the saleswoman's confident assertion that my braids should be brown and *blonde*. Damn you, Confident Saleswoman!

Now I'm back in my apartment. It's 1:30 a.m. on Friday night (or Saturday morning?), and I've been online all day scrambling to order hair in hopes that I can get my twist restyled in black instead of brown/blonde because fifteen people have already made fun of my hair on Instagram. I got the blonde hair braids installed because I was trying to convince myself to try something new. Be fun! Live a little! That blonde hair I have to wear seven months of the year could be me for real! (?) I thought I'd stop worrying about it once it was done. I should've known better than to venture out of my black-to-dark-brown comfort zone. So very disappointing.

I'm not sure why I care so much about those fifteen (and climbing) people and what they have to say about my hair. To be fair, they also hate my dress, but that doesn't make me feel as bad. I'm used to them hating my clothes. But my hair? NO! Why has God forsaken me this way? The thing is, I've conditioned myself to carry a lot of my confidence in my hair. My self-confidence is part hair flips and part tress twirls around my finger. That's how I flirt. It's how Momma makes her money. Clothes I haven't figured out. I'm never sure what I should wear to a fancy event. But hair? I always know exactly what

I want my hair to look like: down and flowing with bangs to frame my face. I never wear my hair up. Never! There have been a few attempts. I've had stylists comb my hair into high ponytails, but as soon as I walk out the door, I pull out the ponytails and apologize to the stylists, saying, "I'm sorry! I just can't. Executive decision." I want to wear a high bun one day, but what I *want* has nothing to do with what I'm comfortable with. A lot of thought has gone into this, which is why I like to think I've figured out my hair. So when someone attacks it, I'm hurt.

When I was a child, hair was my mom's deal. I had no control over it. On weekends she'd make me put two cushions from the couch on the floor in front of her as she sat on the couch on the remaining cushion. She'd have me sit on those cushions on the floor in between her legs, and she'd braid my hair while she watched all the soap operas she'd recorded during the week.

Getting my hair braided was torture. Sitting Indian-style for hours made my fat little legs fall asleep. I'd twist and turn and fall off the cushions just so my mom would be forced to stop combing, pulling, and braiding long enough to let me stand up and sit down again in a different position. In my impatience, I'd reach my little hand up to feel how much hair was left to be braided, which would knock my hair out of place, which would encourage my mom to smack my hand with the comb and tell me to stop it and accept my fate.

There were reprieves. My mom would pause for ten minutes every hour to smoke a cigarette, and I'd get to hop up and down to wake up my legs. When she'd finish her smoke break, we'd both go to pee, and then she'd tell me to stop crying and get back down on the cushions so she could finish.

"How many more," I'd scream through tears and puffy eyes.

"A hundred! Sit down!" my mom would say.

I'd sit back down and make sour faces and wish I'd been born a boy. Sometimes it would take my mom two days to braid my hair, which proves she was taking it easy on me. These days it takes a professional hairstylist about five hours to do the job, and I have a grown-up-size head. I bet if I hadn't complained as much as I did and hadn't driven my mom to need a smoke every hour, she could've finished my kid-size head in about four hours. Maybe even three!

Courtesy of Gabourey Sidibe

Daycare Gabby Yes, there are colored palm trees all over my outfit! You don't know anything about fashion! Though you can't see them in this photo, my socks also have palm trees on them. I'd like credit for that, please and thank you. Also, check out that nose again! I STILL can't even! So cute!

I have to admit something: I was definitely overreacting back then. Did it hurt? Totally. It sucked. (It doesn't hurt anymore because my scalp is now dead with no more life or feeling.) I was a dramatic child, and I was mostly pissed that my brother got to do whatever he wanted while I had to sit with my mom for hours. Just the two of us. I didn't use that time to ask her for advice about crushes or how to make friends, and she didn't teach me anything. I complained, and she watched her soap operas.

I secretly liked watching my mom watch her shows. When I was quiet, it felt like she would forget I was in the room, and braiding became just something she was doing with her hands. It could've been knitting or playing with a yo-yo. She was alone, and she was watching her shows after a long week of work and raising two kids. I was watching her be an adult. A person. Not just a mommy. I'd listen to her talk to the TV screen when Erica Kane's long-lost daughter Kendall showed up on *All My Children.* Or when Viki Lord split from Clint Buchanan and then remarried a year later on *One Life to Live.* I felt like I was getting to spy on who my mom was when her children weren't around. Maybe I was getting to spy into my own future. Maybe I was seeing the woman I'd become . . . a woman with long and silky hair . . .

My mom and I have very different hair. My mom's hair is black, shiny, and easily maintained. Although it's been said a million times by every black person ever, this is supposedly due to some Native American ancestry. Whatever the reason, my mom hit a hereditary hair jackpot. When I was in the first grade, she dyed her hair a dark purplish red, and she wore red clothes to match. This was one of the most exciting times of my life. I thought she was so cool, and she really was. I remember one near-summer day she wore a red trench dress with a matching red-brimmed hat with her perfect purple-red hair curled softly into a bob. With red lipstick. She was so fucking fierce! (She was way too good for my dad!) I couldn't wait to grow up and be her. I wanted purple-red hair, and I wanted all of my clothes to be purple-red, too. And I wanted to live in a purple-red house and drive a purple-red car and live a big purple-red life. That was the dream. I know it sounds childish. But don't you judge me; that's *still* the dream.

My hair, on the other hand, has been rough from birth. I was born with a head full of curly hair: curly, black, and gray. Yes. I was born with gray hair. Tough, wiry, gray hair that couldn't be tamed. My parents figured the gray strands would go away after a while, but no. The older I got, the more gray hair I got. Strangers would stop my mother on the train, and say, "Oh! Ya baby's hair is gray! She must be lucky! That's a blessing." But in school the other kids would say, "Why is ya hair gray? You old! Maybe you cursed!" I hated it—the teasing, not my hair. My hair I loved. When my mom told me that I'd have salt and pepper all over my head by the time I was in my twenties, I couldn't wait. I wanted to look like Lena Horne in her older, graceful stage. Or like Alexandra from *Josie and the Pussycats*. I thought my gray hair made me look distinguished, like a gentlemanly sea captain. Or the wise grandmother tree in *Pocahontas*. I kept hoping that my gray hair would eventually take the form of a lightning bolt in the middle of my head. I felt special—as long as I wasn't in school. In school the feeling of being "special" became the feeling of being "different." Children are assholes and they ruin everything.

In junior high, I compiled a list of all the things people made fun of me for. The point of the list was to see what I could change in order to stop being made fun of. Gray hair seemed like the easiest thing to deal with, so I asked my mom if I could dye my hair. I was sure she'd say no. The year before, when I asked if I could start perming my hair instead of getting it braided, we fought for months before she finally gave in. She'd been wearing her own hair permed in tight Shirley Temple curls with way too much mousse (for staying power). When she relented, she styled my hair in exactly the same way so we looked like twins. Where was the Bureau of Child Welfare then?

My mom seemed to like my gray hair as much as I did, but eventually I convinced her to let me dye it jet-black. The morning after my dye job, I was so excited to go to school. My mom was excited, too! I'd decided that I wouldn't mention what I was planning to my friends and classmates; I'd let them be shocked and amazed by my new hair all on their own. This didn't happen. They didn't notice. I started to drop hints, but still no one noticed. After lunch, I finally blurted out: "Hello! My hair is all black now! No more gray! I dyed it!"

"Oh," my friends responded. "Oh, yeah. It looks nice."

I was pissed.

When I got home, my mom was waiting to hear how my grand hair reveal had gone.

"Did ya friends notice your hair?" she asked, smiling.

"Mom! It's just hair. It doesn't even matter."

"Oh. Okay," she said.

There! Now she was just as disappointed as I was. Children are assholes and they ruin everything.

By the time I was in high school, my mom had stopped caring about my hair altogether. She was fed up with dealing with me and my brother all the time, so she basically threw up the peace sign and yelled, "I'm OUT!" This applied to hair and pretty much everything else. She'd still pay for whatever Ahmed or I needed, but we were allowed to make most of our own decisions and mistakes. We could stay out as late as we wanted, ditch class, and change our hair! My brother dropped out of high school. I made an equally bad decision: I bleached my hair blonde. A bad perm had made my hair short and even more unmanageable than before, so when a friend suggested I bleach it, I was just young and dumb enough to say, "Why not?" My friend, a guy named Calrisian, decided to bleach his hair as well. He was having problems with his parents so he'd left home to live with his older brother. Like me, he had barely any rules to abide by, and it was only a few weeks to summer vacation. Our lives had become a Mad Max movie. We thought, *Fuck it! Let's be blonde!*

He went first. I think we bought (stole) some sort of bleaching paste from the beauty-supply store and put it in his hair. Then Calrisian put it in my hair and combed it down around my face, smoothing it in around my ears. About twenty minutes later, we both held our heads under the showerhead in the bathroom and washed out the bleach. His hair was now bimbo blonde, exactly what he wanted. My hair was now . . . orange, like the fruit. My gray hair had turned a sickly yellow orange and had become even more wiry and untamable. But that wasn't the worst of it.

Did you know that there's hair on your face so short and thin that you can't normally see it? I didn't — until that hair turned bright orange because the bleach my friend combed around my ears had dripped down my face. When it was all rinsed out and blow-dried, my entire head looked like I'd dipped it into a bag of Cheetos. I don't remember how my friends at school reacted to my new hairstyle. It's possible that I blocked it out, in which case, thank you, brain!

I eventually had to shave my face because the orange glow kept attracting moths. As for the orange hair on my head . . . did you know that bleach and chlorine don't mix well? I didn't. I went swimming with my cousins in a pool, and good-bye orange hair, hello green hair! Yes, I now had green hair. I don't remember what I did to get rid of the green hair. (Thank you again, brain!) I assume I just burned it down, collected the insurance money, and then moved to Canada.

Apart from the short-orange-hair episode, I generally wore my hair in braids in high school, but I waited so long in between hairstyles that my real hair would grow under the braid and start to dread up. I started wrapping a bandanna around my head to hide it. The problem: I went to a New York City high school. We had to walk through metal detectors in the lobby, and there were a few gangs so we weren't allowed to wear bandannas. They were called "colors," and there was a "no colors or gang paraphernalia allowed" policy. Do I look like a fucking gang member? It didn't matter. Rules were rules. So every day I'd wear the bandanna in the halls until I got to class. Then I'd wait until my teacher told me to take it off. When the bell rang, I'd tie it back around my head. Some of my teachers would let me keep the bandanna on because they realized I wasn't a gang member—just a sad girl who had yet to figure out her hair. Bless those teachers.

There were girls in my high school who already had weaves. Twenty-five inches of hair flowing down to their asses. These girls didn't wear backpacks to hold their schoolbooks; they used shopping bags from department stores like Macy's. They had Gucci and Louis Vuitton purses filled with rolled-up spiral notebooks and makeup. They swung their beautiful long hair and expensive but probably fake purses down the hall. I struggled behind with my tough short hair hidden under a scarf, toting a misshapen backpack filled with all my textbooks and at least three notebooks, looking like the Hunchback of Notre Dame on his way to ring that bell. We walked the same halls and were probably the same age, but we were light-years apart.

I was twenty-four when I finally got my first weave. It was a gift from the hairstylist on the set of *Precious*. I loved it! It made doing my hair so easy. I'd flat-iron my weave, comb it down, and leave the house, swinging my hair just like those girls in high school. I'd toss my head and twirl my weave around my finger, and that's when I started to figure out how to draw confidence from my hair. All I had to do was give up the ability to scratch my scalp. (It's impossible to even touch my scalp with two layers of hair—mine and someone else's—and a net to keep everything down.)

Weaves have been a godsend. Shooting for film and television requires hair continuity. I spend weeks filming a ton of scenes in the same outfit, and my hair has to be exactly the same as well. On average, I probably get my hair done six times a day. If my own hair was flat-ironed or curled that many times, it would fall out. But if the weave falls out, they just sew in a new one. I always wear them when I'm working, and they make me feel normal. (I just wish that word *normal* didn't hold so much weight for me.)

My gray hair has been gone for years. I can't explain what happened. In my twenties I suddenly started to notice less and less of it until there wasn't any at all. Perhaps I've run out of luck or wisdom. Maybe I'm the real-life Benjamin Button and I'm growing backward so the older I get, the younger and more beautiful I appear to be. That's explanation enough for me.

My hair and I have been through a lot (it's been on fire twice). There are many more hair battles to come, but I know my strength and beauty start at the roots. I've realized that black women have the most beautiful hair: long hair, weaves or natural; bobs, cut straight or asymmetrical; braids; dreads; Afros; shaved bald; faded with a flat top. Our hair can be anything! Choose a color, choose a texture, and our hair can do it. There's an entire Black Woman Hair Universe of Possibilities. I've always felt like I was on the outside of that universe looking in and longing to be bold enough to be a part of it. My hair has been through so much trauma that I'm afraid to venture out into the vast terrain of the beauty my hair could be. I'm working on it! I'm just starting to figure out the wonder of each curly tress.

6

MAKE A WISH

Do you sing like your mom?
— fans of my mother's

'VE BEEN DOING THIS THING with my mom where I ask her really personal questions. I'm no longer a teenager so I see the value in her words and experiences. Her grandmother was born a slave! My mom's filled with interesting things to say. I always feel like a real adult when I sit across from her and ask her horribly intrusive questions and then she answers them honestly. For this conversation, we were sitting around my dining-room table in my small yet expensive and kind of fancy apartment in New York City. The last time the two of us sat at this table, we were trying to mend fences after a fight. I had hurt my mother's feelings, but apologizing wasn't enough since she thought I'd hurt her on purpose. The fight had dragged on for months and was still pretty alive. I remember yelling at her, "You see these walls? You see these ceiling-to-floor windows? This apartment that I live in alone? It's EXPENSIVE! I pay for it all by myself, and when you need my help, I pay for your walls, too! I don't have the time to plan out something terrible to do to you! I'm not plotting on how to purposely hurt your feelings. I'm a grown-up and I'm too busy working to keep roofs over our heads to take the time to try to hurt you!"

That fight was pretty intense, but on this day Mom and I were fine. Neither of us were mad, and I was realizing how little time we actually got to spend with each other. I thought, *Now's a great time to get to know her as a person instead of just a mom.*

"Do you think you have more money than your parents had?" I asked.

"Definitely," she answered. "Daddy hauled lumber and MaDear cleaned white folks' houses for a dollar a day. I didn't know we were poor, though. MaDear would get stuff from the people she worked for. They'd give her a broken TV or broken chairs, and we would fix them up. MaDear made our couch! And Daddy was so smart. He gave the whole neighborhood electricity. Daddy fixed a broken TV, and we were the only family in the neighborhood who had one. People used to come over every night to watch. House was always full of people so . . . I didn't know we were poor. We were popular. I had a great time!"

I envied her childhood. I envy her adulthood sometimes, too. Once when Mom and I were in a different fight, different yet the same as that other fight (Moms! Am I right?), she said to me, "I guess it's harder to raise children in New York City. I had a great life growing up in Georgia. It's too bad you didn't get to experience happiness like I did as a child."

Aunt Dorothy was my mother's sister. She was the only person I knew who had a staircase in her house like people on TV. The rest of my mother's family, who lived in one-level homes in the South, didn't have staircase money, but Aunt Dorothy did.

As for us, when we left my father, we went from a three-bedroom apartment to just one room in that house, so the staircase turned out to be beside the point. My brother and I weren't really allowed out into the rest of the house, so our one room was where we lived. My mom bought a TV and a microwave for our room. It dawned on me that finally we were poor. Actually poor! No matter how little I asked of my mother, no matter how much I worried, we were poor anyway. My nightmares had come true.

I was always worried about money as a child. At the age of seven, I'd be really excited to go get the mail, and I complained that the only people who got any mail were my parents. My dad joked that he should put the electric bill in my name. I didn't get my dad's humor back then as it so rarely showed its head. I panicked. I had never thought about paying bills before, but all of a sudden I was responsible for keeping the electricity on in the entire apartment! Again, I wasn't. But I was forever changed and made aware that everything had a cost.

While I didn't yet know that we were poor, I knew we weren't rich because we weren't white. Back then I thought that being rich was only for white people and Michael Jackson. We lived in a three-bedroom apartment with two bathrooms and a terrace in Brooklyn. Of course we weren't poor!

Duh! But I started asking how much everything cost. I was worried about what we could afford. I stopped begging for things, and started asking, "Can you afford to buy me this?" while ready to accept the answer if it was no. (I don't remember if I ever got an answer at all. I probably didn't.) When my parents asked what I wanted for Christmas or my birthday, I would comb through the Toys"R"Us catalog in the weekly paper for toys I didn't necessarily want, but that I felt were inexpensive enough. I was just doing my part to keep us from being poor. Maybe I *am* a good person?

After we moved, I blamed our new poverty on my father, who was still in our old three-bedroom apartment that was basically a mansion compared to our new standard of living, and I was pissed. As an adult, as soon as I figured out I didn't want to grow up in Brooklyn anyway, I assigned less blame on my father, at least moving-wise, but when I was a child, it was really comforting to place blame on him for our situation. I had worried myself into believing that if I wasn't selfish I could keep my family from living on the streets. I'd conned myself when I was just a child into being responsible for an entire family. Fuck that noise. It was really nice to come face-to-face with my fear and get to blame it on someone else. I truly hated my father then, and that hate brought me a calming joy for a while. A peace of mind. It wasn't my fault. It was his. Now I can just go back to being a kid!

Then my mom quit her job as a teacher. Technically, she went on a leave of absence. I can't remember my outward reaction to this, but my inside reaction was a constant scream of "ARE YOU FUCKING CRAZY? YOU QUIT YOUR JOB????????!!!!!!" I can't imagine I said that aloud, but I was worried again. When we left my father, I assumed I was going to have just one parent supporting us now. My mom. What the fuck was that one parent doing quitting her job? She was going to make money singing in the subway and maybe get discovered there. My uncle Roger had been a subway performer for years at that point. He was a big man with a powerful voice. Uncle Roger played guitar while singing blues covers and Motown standards. He made his own schedule, was his own boss, and raised his three children pretty well. After sometimes going to sing with him in the subway and seeing that he made enough money to survive, my mother was going to follow her brother Roger's example and do it on her own.

The great thing about this very scary plan was that my mom is a phenomenal singer. The terrible thing about this plan was that not every phenomenal singer gets discovered. I was worried my mom didn't have enough that was special to set her apart from all the other great singers. She had two kids, a broken marriage, and lived in her sister's guest room. That's not how Whitney Houston started her career. I was very pessimistic. I didn't believe in my mother then because I didn't believe in dreams coming true then. The irony of me as a grown-up being a fat black woman on prime-time television isn't lost on me. I'll get to that, but first I'll remind you that being on TV wasn't my dream then. At the time, it seemed like my mom was expecting a miracle, and I just didn't believe in those.

My mom pretty much decided her own hours, and she made money exclusively in cash tips. On average, she made between $200 and $300 a shift, and worked between four and five days a week. So that's $800 or $900 a week. This was as much as she'd made in a month working for the New York City Public

Schools. But this did nothing to alleviate my fears. I was afraid because she had no insurance. She couldn't work every day because her instrument was her throat. If she sang every day, she'd go hoarse and be unable to sing, meaning she'd make no money at all. I lived in constant fear of her getting sick and losing her voice. Who would take care of us? Certainly not my dad. As far as I was concerned, he no longer had any responsibility toward us. We weren't family anymore.

My mom paid rent to my aunt Dorothy. But Dorothy was often annoyed with us. I didn't put it past her to kick us out of her house. As an adult, I don't think she would have, but as a kid, I couldn't and didn't trust her. I knew she didn't want us around. I can't say I blame her. I was a smart-mouthed asshole of a kid, and my brother was an angry child who drew patterns in her carpet with dish soap.

My mom would take us with her when she sang in the subway on weekends and in the evenings because my aunt didn't like us in the house by ourselves. Ahmed and I would sit together on a bench on the platform and watch people commute to and from work. Commute to and from their homes. Commute to and from fancier lives than ours. My mother could always command a crowd to stand around and watch her in awe. Some people would miss their trains to listen to her sing their favorite song. People would dance and sing along. She made them forget about their long days in the office. She made people happy. I watched her work her magic on everyone. Everyone but me. I watched her and I was scared. I was scared of more than just being evicted by my aunt, more than just my mom getting sick. Watching all those people put money in my mom's bag as she sang made me worry that someone was watching her and waiting to knock her down and steal that money from her. From us. I was afraid that she would get hurt. I was also afraid that one day I'd have to do what she was doing. That I'd have to grow up and become a singer in the subway like her but that I wouldn't be as good as her because I wasn't as good as her. That's a lot to worry about as a child.

If my brother was worried like me, he didn't show it. I think he thought we were doing pretty well; he could see the money she made. Also, Ahmed was super into trains as a kid, so he loved watching the trains come in and out of the stations. A lot of times, he would get on a train, ride around for a few hours, and then come back. This was before cell phones. Can you even imagine a nine-year-old riding the subway by himself for hours at a time? They don't make kids like they used to. Ahmed and I were scrappy! I didn't dig being on trains as much, so I would wander around the train station. Whenever our mom played Penn Station, I would stroll from store to store checking out magazines and books. I usually brought my own books or my homework, but I was always in the market for a new book to read. There was a bookstore down there called Penn Books, and I loved it. I was in there all the time, and the people who worked there would turn a blind eye whenever I picked up a book and sat on the floor to read it. It was quiet there, which I liked. I couldn't hear any trains, I couldn't hear any crowds, and I couldn't hear my mother singing to pay the rent. As long as I couldn't hear it, I didn't have to admit that it was happening.

If Ahmed and I stood where my mom could see us, and we could see her, eventually people would notice us and come over and want to talk about our mom. I think that made my brother feel kind of famous, but I hated it. I have always had a hard time with strangers, as I've definitely mentioned, but strangers who just wanted to talk about how wonderful and talented my mom was were especially unwelcome. They'd say, "Your mom is incredible!" and I'd reply, "Yeah." It felt like I should say, "Thank you," but I knew I had nothing to do with my mom's talent so that felt wrong. "Yeah" was the end of the conversation. Also, speaking as a grown-up, *Um . . . so?* Like you think Lourdes is just a little bit tired of hearing how amazing her mom Madonna is? I feel this is something only a child of a celebrity understands. People would talk to me about how amazing my mom was and how they didn't know why she wasn't signed to a label or on the radio and how she made them so happy and how her music changed their lives. What was I supposed to do with that? I was proud of my mom, but I still went to bed in the same room she and my brother did and was too scared to ask her for money for a school trip because I was afraid we could be put out on the streets. (Actually, now that I think about it, Lourdes probably has it pretty good on the money-anxiety front.)

My mom didn't always take us with her. A lot of times, she was still at work when we got home from school. Ahmed and I didn't have keys to our aunt's house so we would stand outside ringing the doorbell and praying that someone was home. A few times, no one was, so we'd stand on the steps outside waiting for what felt like hours. Nothing makes you feel poorer than waiting outside in the cold of winter for your single mom to show up and let you in. We didn't know the neighbors well enough to knock on their doors and ask them if we could wait there. My brother was always down to do that, but I was never willing to burden anyone else with us latchkey kids without a key. To make things worse, I *always* had to pee, so . . . ya know. Uncle Roger lived five blocks away, so occasionally we would walk over to his house and stay there until my mother got home. Eventually, Mom gave us her house key, but we couldn't let my aunt know we were in her house alone. I guess she thought we'd break something or maybe we'd like join a cult and sacrifice a body in her kitchen. I'm not sure what she was afraid of. Maybe just of letting a nine- and ten-year-old alone in a three-story house. I'm actually too jaded to know if that's something to be worried about or not. Either way, the worst thing we ever did was fight over the TV. We weren't allowed to pick up the phone in case it was Dorothy checking to see if we were alone. My mom came up with a signal for us. If the phone rang once, stopped, and then started ringing again, it was Mom, calling us to ask what we wanted for dinner and say that she was on her way home. Wasn't the world crazy before cell phones?

As an adult, I see that I shouldn't have worried so much. I should've had some hope that our situation would get better. I should've believed that one day my mom would be discovered singing down there in the subway. She knew how to walk into a room and make people fall for her. Even if that room was Grand Central Station. She believed in a bigger life for herself and her children. She was truly happy when she was out there singing for an audience that would become her fans. I'm sure she had rough moments when she didn't know how she would take care of the three of us, but she never let Ahmed and me see her worry. She believed in her magic. I wished then that I was more like my mother. I wish I was more like her now.

My mom wasn't wrong about things working out. Soon after she began singing in the subway, she started getting hired to do private gigs. She would sing at weddings, bar mitzvahs, corporate parties, birthday parties, and whatever else people wanted to celebrate. This was a good thing because she made more money doing private gigs. Not just tips like in the subway.

Once she was hired to sing at a fair for families who lived in homeless shelters on Long Island. She took Ahmed and me with her, and we met the families and played games with them. My mom sang and everyone enjoyed her. I saw that our situation could be much worse. My mom reminded me that day to be grateful instead of fearful, and it worked for a while.

Once my mom got a call from the Make-A-Wish Foundation. There was a girl with a terminal illness who'd seen my mom singing in the subway, and now it was her dying wish to hang out with her. Mom met with her and took her singing in the subway. The girl was a few years older than Ahmed or I. She was a teenager, she was dying, and she just wanted to sing with my mom before she died. I remember Mom calmly and cheerfully agreeing to this last wish over the phone. She didn't seem saddened by it. I was ready to throw myself off a roof just so I didn't have to think about a dying kid, but Mom saw this as an opportunity to share her gift with a fan and make her happy. She always sees opportunity where I see only fear and death. I stayed awake for days thinking about that girl who in her last days probably liked Mom more than I did. I never spoke to my mom about her. I didn't ask all the questions I wanted to ask to alleviate my fears. I remember the girl dying. As of a conversation I had with Mom ten minutes ago, one of those conversations where I ask her really personal questions, she doesn't remember the girl at all. But Mom wasn't surprised to hear that hanging out with her was someone's dying wish. I can't tell if that's being aware of one's gift or evidence of a severely narcissistic ego. It's probably a pretty thin line.

7

PARADE OF UGLY

*I'm already planning my wardrobe for when I'm
a director. #NotoriousB.I.G.shirtseveryday.*

— my Twitter

N THE SEVENTH GRADE I had a windbreaker from Con-
way. It was a baby blue and white Perry Ellis jacket with a
zip hood in the collar. It was my first name-brand article of
clothing. It wasn't until a kid in my class told me that the jacket
was "designer" that I bothered to read the name written across
the back. But even I knew right away that this jacket was something special, in that color and with that hideaway hood. I'd
wear it with jeans that were too big with rips at the crotch
I'd cover over with iron-on cartoon patches, an oversize shirt I
borrowed from my mom, and these gross, slouchy Lugz boots
I'd asked for for Christmas in the fifth grade and was still growing into.

I loved that jacket. I wore it until the ninth grade when my mom finally made me throw it out because it had holes and tears, and because women were stopping my mom and me in the street to offer me their own secondhand clothing. They thought we were too poor to afford a decent, clean girl's jacket. My mom was mortified. I, on the other hand, was just trying to find my style. I wanted to be a tomboy. I wasn't really a tomboy, but my best friend at the time was a pretty, skinny, black Puerto Rican girl with a big butt who was super girlie. It didn't really make sense to compete with her, so I went in a different direction. That direction was dressing like a wayward hobo. In my twenties I realized I no longer wanted to dress like a hobo lumberjack, so I invested in a new feminine look. I wore denim miniskirts with jewel-bedazzled pockets, peasant blouses, and white socks with pink Converse sneakers that I bought for five dollars on eBay. Most of my new clothes were pink because I thought the color made me seem more dainty and brightened my dark skin. Also, I wore shades *all* the time. Day or night, rain or shine. And I'd coordinate the colors to match my shirts. I still borrowed my mom's shirts, but I unbuttoned them so I could show off my bra because I was very sexy. Duh. Clearly I was still trying to find my style.

When I started going to premieres for *Precious,* I shopped for dresses at Torrid, a plus-size clothing store. I bought prom dresses. For the Sundance Film Festival, which is cool and casual, I chose a bubble-gum-pink tube dress with pockets in the skirt, a black shrug, and black knee boots. I walked the carpet by myself, clutching an oversize Gucci purse that Sarah, the film's producer, had given me. For Cannes, I found a black dress with a ton of ruffles. I paired it with another shrug, a fake pearl necklace I borrowed from Mom, and kitten heels. I blended in that night and my entire outfit cost $120!

For a Cannes press conference with the actors in the film, I was told that the dress code was "casual." That was a lie. Every waking moment at Cannes is black-tie, but I didn't know that.

Photo Op You DON'T know pressure until you've had to stand directly in between Paula Patton and Mariah Carey in clothes you bought from a mall and Payless shoes. What do you know about the struggle?! I'm a fucking SURVIVOR!

I wore the only heels I could walk in, a pair of brown wedges, and a green floral-print dress that I thought was too short, so I put on jean capris underneath. If you think that sounds bad, keep in mind that I had to stand between Mariah Carey and Paula Patton for every picture. There! Now you know it wasn't just bad, it was a nightmare. But the day wasn't all horrible. Later I met Debbie Harry while wearing a T-shirt with her face on it. Fashion WIN!

At both the Sundance and Cannes premieres, I was scared to death. Paula and Mariah were both so pretty, and both had an entire team of people to make sure they looked good. Stylists, assistants, hairstylists, makeup artists, publicists. I had none of those people. I didn't have any money to pay for all that.

But I was the face of our film. I played the title character, so I had to show up no matter how inappropriate my outfit. At Sundance, my costar Mo'Nique kindly had her hair and makeup artist prepare me for the premiere, but the rest of the time I made myself up even though I had no clue how. I felt like a contest winner—in a bad way. Like I didn't really belong on the red carpets, but I'd sold the most raffle tickets, so the powers that be were allowing me to feel fancy for a night, but in the morning I'd have to go back to working the phones at the call center . . . or something.

When *Precious* was picked up for distribution by Lionsgate, I'd already won a few awards and was on the verge of being nominated for more. The company hired a stylist to dress me for the rest of the awards season and paid for hair and makeup as well. I finally had a team to make sure I looked presentable the next time I had to stand next to Mariah! The stylist, Linda, and her assistant met me at my hotel in LA. They brought a

ton of clothes to my room, and I tried everything on. Linda
didn't know me and didn't really know my style. I figured that
was fine, because I didn't really know my style yet, either. (I
still missed my Perry Ellis jacket!)

Linda asked me what I'd seen in magazines that I liked. She
asked what I wanted to look like, what kind of dresses I liked,
what colors I wanted to wear. I didn't know how to answer any
of those questions. I'd never opened a magazine and thought,
I want to look like this! The closest I'd ever come was watching
Moesha as a teenager and wishing I could dress like Moesha's
best friend, Kim. She was a big girl, and so was I, but she always had a boyfriend, so I figured that I should dress like her.
Somehow I knew that saying this to Linda — saying "Moesha's
best friend" to a woman whose other clients included Cameron Diaz and Helen Hunt — was the wrong answer. So I said
the only thing I knew for sure: "I don't need a dress that will
stand out. I'll do that anyway. I just want to look like I belong."

She seemed optimistic that I'd fit in. She suggested that I
start buying magazines and paying attention to fashion trends
and saving pictures of dresses that I liked. So, yes, this is the
story of what it's like to choose a dress for a glamorous award
ceremony. You're probably thinking, *How hard could that be?*
Sounds like the most fun part! Hold ON. Not so fast. Have you
forgotten about the *Fashion Police*? Have you forgotten about
the blogs and the fashion reporters? Have you forgotten the
Denim Debacle that Justin Timberlake and Britney Spears
wore to the American Music Awards in 2001? I haven't. I had
a discussion about that outfit at a dinner party *last night*. The
world hasn't forgotten and it never will. What's worse is that I
thought those outfits were dope. That's right. I would've been

all the way onboard with that decision. This is why it was dangerous for me to flip through magazines for trends and dresses I liked.

I didn't know it then, but my personal fashion icon was and is Lena Dunham. I've been in the same room as Lena about eight times, and I've only really had one conversation with her. It was the day after the 2014 Emmys. At the show I'd worn this beautiful, flowing, orange Octavio Carlin dress that took a team of red-carpet scientists to tug and straighten (my bra made an appearance in every picture). Before the Emmys even started, I'd ripped the skirt and broken my makeup compact. I was looking around for a place I could stash my heels, already feeling like a contest winner, when I saw Lena. She was across the room wearing a collared blouse with capped sleeves tucked into a huge, poofy, pink Giambattista Valli skirt. I overheard someone nearby state her opinion of the outfit, but it wasn't my opinion, so it was wrong and really not worth repeating. In that instant I knew I had found my hero.

Lena's skirt was so big and fluffy! I imagined what it might feel like to sit on it in one of those hard theater chairs. Maybe it was like sitting on pillows or, even better, marshmallows. It was at least four kinds of pink. Her hair was freshly bleached blonde, and she made me think of a baby sitting on a cloud of cotton candy. She looked fearless. Confident. If she felt like a contest winner, she didn't show it. She didn't seem positive that she belonged there, either, but her attitude said, "Fuck you! I'm here, and this is my skirt, bitches!" It was magic, and ever since, I've gotten a thrill from seeing her on a red carpet.

Here's the thing. Lena doesn't just have confidence. Confidence is easier than what I see in Lena. I see something that says, "I know what I am and what I'm worth, and if you don't like it, you don't exist. Also, my skirt is PINK!" It's not confidence. It's privilege. Now usually a black girl talking about a white girl having privilege is a commentary on race and class. Not this time. This time I'm just talking about dresses. Lena seems to have granted herself immunity from all of the bad shit, stress, and worry that accompanies a red carpet. It's like she wakes up and checks her calendar, and says, "Gee! The Golden Globes are this weekend. I wanna wear . . . YELLOW!" And somehow a yellow dress shows up, and come that weekend, she's on the carpet in a yellow dress thinking, *Fuck, yeah! YELLOW!* while somewhere in the background I'm sweating with one heel in my hand, trying to find my seat, and hoping that my dress photographed well so that those bitches on *Fashion Police* don't talk shit about me.

Before I found Lena for my style guru, I didn't really know what I wanted to wear. But my stylist Linda knew, and she had the ability to pull out some really fancy dresses that my prom dresses could never compete with. So I let her make most of my fashion decisions for me. I thought that most of the dresses I wore were really pretty, but I can't say that I wore anything that was *my* style. Eventually, I found a stylist who specialized in plus-size style. Marcy Guevara-Prete is a beautiful, plus-size girlie girl who believes that every woman, regardless of size, should feel special all the time. She wears clothes I want to wear. Dresses with tulip skirts that fly out when she spins around. Cute leather boots with a matching leather vest and big pretty jewelry. She understands my plus-size body and helps me dress it in clothing that I'd actually pick out for myself.

I like to think red carpets are like that '90s TV show *American Gladiators*. The show matched amateur athletes against professional bodybuilders with names like Nitro, Turbo, and Hawk in games of strength and agility. I am the amateur athlete. The red carpet is the test of agility. Cameron Diaz is Nitro, Penelope Cruz is Turbo, and Jennifer Lopez is Hawk (obviously). Armed with my stylist Marcy, my confidence, and the ability to quickly pick it up when it falls, I run as fast as I can through the gauntlet of actors, interviewers, and photographers — straight to the prize. The prize is the bottle of champagne I'm going to allow myself to drink on my way to my seat.

Now I don't actually know Lena or what she's thinking on the red carpet. I could be completely wrong about her. After all, people look at me and see a beacon of self-confidence even though I'm nervous and feel like a freak a lot of the time and worry that Giuliana Rancic and Billy Bush can smell my fear. I get out of that SUV, I step onto the red carpet, and I'm standing in line behind the Amy Adamses, the Jennifer Lawrences, and the Kate Hudsons. They're all so beautiful, with unimpressed faces and hand-sewn dresses that I could never fit into and will never be sexy enough to pull off. None of them are sweating. My confidence falls and crashes at my feet, and I wish I'd had one more drink before getting in the car. I never understand addiction more than when I'm on a red carpet. I just want to be numb.

But just when I'm thinking, *Never again!* and I am afraid I'll have a panic attack, I see Lena. She's wearing something that I wouldn't choose for myself, but it's a pretty color and she's smiling. She looks happy. She's like a lighthouse. She becomes *my* beacon of confidence. She's talented, and she's there because she's earned it. Like me. They don't give out tickets at Chuck E. Cheese's to award shows. I'm invited because I do good work and I choose cool projects. Seeing her reminds me of that. I remember to feel pretty, talented, and at home on the red carpet in my big, flowing, soon-to-be-ripped dress. By the way, when I became a director, I truly did wear a Biggie shirt, paired with an African-print skirt, every single day. There's nothing more fashion-forward than being the fucking BOSS!

8

A DOOR OF ONE'S OWN

Why do you hate me?
Because you're ugly.
— *Welcome to the Dollhouse*

'M NOT A HUGE FAN of Christmas the way most people
are. People love it for all the lights and pretty decorations and
family time filled with old traditions. Jesus or Kwanzaa-God,
whoever that might be. Christmas is for families, but as you
know by now, my family is very small. My mom has a ton of
siblings, but they all live in the South. My father . . . well, you
know, his family's in Africa, and he's not invited to our nontra-
ditional, nonholiday holidays for the time being. No. I'm not a
big fan of Christmas. It just reminds me of what I don't have
anymore.

When Ahmed and I were kids, and my parents were still
married to each other, Christmas was pretty amazing. I'd start
begging my mom to put up our plastic tree in the living room

next to the terrace sometime around Halloween. About a week before Christmas, the tree would finally go up, and my mom, brother, and I would decorate it together while my dad was out driving his cab. Late at night, around 2 a.m., my dad would pick up my brother and me, and take us to see the Rockefeller Center Christmas tree. Ahmed and I would fight over who got to sit up front. Ahmed always won. The city was quiet and the tree was beautiful. My dad would make an empty promise to take us skating during the daytime, and then we'd get back in the car, and he'd drive us to White Castle for tiny burgers and onion rings (onion rings were a delicacy to me as a child).

The weekend before Christmas, my dad would drive us all to a mall so that my mom could buy us Christmas gifts. Believing in Santa Claus was for other families. Sometimes I'd help my mom wrap the gifts. We were in on what we were getting so it wasn't a big deal.

On Christmas Eve, my mom would let us open one gift, and then we'd go to bed as early as possible in hopes that Christmas Day would come faster than most days. In the morning we'd have to wait until my parents woke up to open our gifts, so my brother and I would make as much noise as possible, and then we'd resort to poking and shaking them until they got out of bed. We'd tear open the gifts that we'd been waiting to open since we went shopping for them. There were always another one or two great presents we didn't know about. My mom made sure to keep a few of our gifts a secret from us so we'd still have surprises on Christmas morning. Later in the day, my mom would take us to my uncle's house, and we'd collect more gifts there. Those were our traditions.

My dad had a tradition of his own. He would buy himself a

Hess toy truck every year and forbid us to touch it. I'm serious. My grown-up father would buy himself a toy, and he wouldn't let us, his children, play with it. I always waited for him to go to work so I could have it to myself. But he always knew, so he started hiding it before he left. That made it into a game for me. I'd find it, play with it, and put it back before he got home. I played with it because . . . fuck him. It's a toy. My right to play with it was certainly more important than his right to have something for himself, right?

After my parents separated, we stopped taking holidays seriously in my family. Thanksgiving was no exception. After my parents split, my mother, brother, and I have always found some place other than my mom's apartment to be for Thanksgiving. It used to be my aunt Dorothy's until she moved to Florida. Then it became my mother's cousin's not far from where we lived in Harlem. For a couple of years, I made a tradition with my high school best friend, Crystal, and we cooked together, but that died out as well. So I was back at my mom's apartment. This meant a baked chicken, rice, and a weird peach cobbler with toast for a crust. This also meant that we three would each grab a plate whenever we felt like it; that we'd each take that plate to a separate room, usually in front of a TV; and that we'd each stay as far away from one another as you can stay in a two-bedroom apartment, my mom on her bed in the living room, my brother in his room, and me in mine. We never sat together to eat. Almost never have we eaten at the same time.

To understand how we got to this point, you have to understand a bit about New York real estate. Shit is expensive.

My mom had to pay Dorothy eight hundred dollars a month for our small room with two twin beds. At first, Ahmed and I switched off sleeping with Mom. But eventually she decided I was too big to share a twin bed. I wasn't too old. I was just too big. So I slept alone, and Ahmed and Mom shared a bed. Our worlds revolved around four hundred square feet. Ahmed and I did our homework in the same room, and we went to bed after fighting over Nintendo in the same room. We lived closer together than ever, and we grew further apart. Familiarity breeds contempt, and we got so we couldn't stand one another.

We lived with my aunt Dorothy for two years before we moved into a studio apartment on the twenty-eighth floor of a building in West Harlem. We had an amazing view of Riverside Park, downtown Manhattan, and New Jersey. It was a subsidized-housing apartment building, which means that the government alleviated some of the housing cost, but the building was privately owned. The rent for our studio pie in the sky was probably around $1,200 when we moved in, but because of the government assistance, my mom paid around $350 a month. If we lived in the projects, we would've paid less.

My brother wanted us to move to the Lillian Wald projects on the Lower East Side of Manhattan. He lobbied for it because all of his friends lived there. I disagreed, but I also understood. All of my friends lived there, too. I had a lot of super-fun times in the projects across the street from my junior high school. (I went to Junior High 22, usually screamed "TWENTY-TWO!!" while walking around the basketball courts with friends.) We would hang out all night in the park or the handball court in Baruch Houses across the street and were always bound to run into people we knew. But I was worried that if we actually lived in the projects my family would never get out. It's not rare to see a family living in the same project neighborhood for three generations or even under the same project apartment roof for that long. I know of a couple that met when they were living in the same project building. They fell in love and got married but still lived in separate apartments on different floors with their own families because even together they didn't make enough money to move out. Instead, they were both on a waiting list for their own project apartment. Most of my friends from the projects still live there today. I say this without judgment, as I know we were one missed rent payment away from being put out on our asses from our subsidized-housing apartment.

Anyway, the three of us still shared one room, but now we were sleeping in a bunk bed. Mom and Ahmed shared the bottom bunk, and I slept on the top. Apart from the bunk bed, we had a couch, a dresser, and a table with our TV and VCR and Super Nintendo on it. We had one chair that I'd sit in to do my homework and look out at the skyline.

There was no dinnertime. Ahmed and I mostly waited until my mom got home to eat. She'd either bring food or cook at around eight o'clock at night. We'd watch *Jenny Jones* at 11 p.m., and then we'd play Super Mario Kart. At midnight we'd watch the Empire State Building shut off its lights. (It doesn't do that anymore. Now the lights stay on all night.) We lived like that for five long years. We didn't have a bedtime; we didn't even have a curfew. As long as my mom knew where we were, we could stay out all night if we wanted to, and we did. If we didn't come home, it meant that whoever was home had more room to stretch out. We didn't have rules or structure because we literally had no space for them. The only alone time we ever had was in the bathroom—and even that wasn't completely private. We knew everything about one another. Ahmed and Alice knew when my period started (March 9, the day Notorious B.I.G. died. I don't know why I needed to tell you that, but I did). They knew when I had my first kiss. And they knew when I had a horrible day at school and couldn't stop crying in class. It was awful.

When I was sixteen, a two-bedroom apartment opened up in our building, and we were next on the waiting list. Alice, no stranger to sacrifices, gave Ahmed and me each a room, and put a daybed in the living room for herself. She didn't want to make either of us share a room ever again. She said that we were teenagers and needed our own space. I don't know if I would've been able to do that if I was in her position, but then again, she's a saint and I'm (still) not.

We didn't have any structure or curfews in the new apartment; it was too late for that. In two years I'd start helping with the rent. We didn't have a table to eat at together, so we had no family meals, no traditions, no rituals. But there were walls between us now. Now we had doors. I shut mine and locked it until I was ready to leave. All of my secrets remained mine for the first time since I was nine years old.

I moved out on my own at the age of twenty-five. If you think that's old, keep in mind that this is New York City. *Shit is expensive!* My mom moved into my old room and finally had her own door to close for the first time in many years. A part of me wishes that life could've been different for Alice. She never dated after leaving Ibnou. Ahmed would've hated that, but I always wished she had. I wish she'd found a soul mate who could've provided a stable life for her. Undying love and devotion. Financial security. A retirement plan. Prettier children. But I know now that's not what Alice wanted. All she's ever wanted is to be happy, and because Alice gets what Alice wants, she is happy. I often think that my family is too small to be a family. There's just three of us. We're more like three people with the same DNA who all lived together once. Like roommates. But Alice and Ahmed are my entire world. I worry more about them than I worry about myself. I keep my ringer on at night in case they need me. I care about them so much that it infuriates me. I pay their rent before I pay my own. As much as I want to pretend that seeing the two of them for the holidays doesn't really matter because we don't have any traditions, it warms my heart to spend time with them. Ugh! I sound like an Olsen twins movie or something. But I mean it. I love visiting them. I love knowing that my mom misses me. I love crawling into bed with her and listening to her tell me how great she is and how much her fans love her.

This year I went home to that two-bedroom apartment to have Thanksgiving with Alice and Ahmed, who lives there still. Since my mom moved into my old bedroom, the living-room furniture has changed. There's a dining-room table with chairs, and there's an armchair and a couch. I asked if we could all sit at that table and eat together. We'd never done that. We did. We all sat together, we held hands as Alice prayed over the food, and then we ate. It was nice even if it didn't really make us a closer family. But we're not as fractured as I sometimes think. We're all we have, yes, but we're enough.

9

OBITUARY

*The only truthful bit of this "article" is that my name
is Gabourey Sidibe. Even that is debatable.*

— my Twitter

AN OLD FRIEND FROM ELEMENTARY school texted me
and asked if I had heard that I was dead. "Did you hear
about your death?" is how she put it. I responded sar-
castically, "No. Please, do tell." "You had a fatal asthma attack."
"Oh, shit! Then what happened?" "You died. Are you okay? I
saw it on Facebook. Want me to send the link to you?" "Oh,
yes! Please!" And then she sent a link to an article about my
death to my Facebook page. Did this bitch not know I was being sarcastic? I hate that sarcasm is hard to convey in a text.
There should be a special font for sarcasm so people can tell
when I'm being an asshole. Of course I'd heard!

This is week five of my friends and family texting or calling me to find out if I'm dead. The report has been circulat-

ing throughout all the social media. I've seen it on both my Instagram and my Twitter, but Facebook is where it got started.
Facebook! You know, that social-media site you use to spy on
your ex and figure out at election time which of your family members are racist. Everything anyone has ever written on
Facebook has to be 100 percent true. If not, Mark Zuckerberg
has to punch a sloth in the face. He doesn't want to, but those
are the rules. (You can tell this is sarcasm, right?) At first, the
Gabby-is-dead article was from a surely reputable online news
site called Can't Stop Hip-Hop Worldwide (I'm pretty sure I
heard that Diane Sawyer once interned there). According to
them, I was filming a scene for an upcoming movie in which I
played a detective. The scene required me to run, and during
a take, I stopped running and motioned for someone to help
me. I was experiencing shortness of breath. I guess my big fat
heart couldn't take it. The ambulance was called but I "expired
en route to the hospital" of a fatal asthma attack. My friends
and family are devastated by the sudden loss. Such a shame. I
was so young and so beloved. I should've known better than to
be fat and run at the same time. I was so foolish to think that
I could have it all. There's no date or location in the article,
so it's unclear when and where I died. Even if I do something
publicly to make it known that I'm still among the living, the
article will spawn Gabby-is-dead conspiracy junkies unto eternity. If you read the news today, you assume it happened last
night, so even if I tweeted something at 7 p.m. yesterday like
"Hi! I'm alive! Stop asking!" you figure I probably died right
afterward. If you read the news tomorrow, no tweet of mine
will stop you from being sure I died right after posting it. I'd
better be careful. Death's a'comin'!

While it was obviously jarring to see my name in a poorly written article about my death, I know that this is just one of those things that happen to celebrities. It comes with the territory. Famous people get free clothes, they get instant reservations and a good table at fancy restaurants, and they get false reports about their deaths. It's happened to friends of mine. It didn't bother me that much at first. Then it moved from Facebook to Twitter. Here and there, people would tweet me and ask if I was okay. They'd extend their condolences to my family. Some knew it was a hoax so they wanted me to "clear it up." How? By being alive? I ignored these requests because I figured that even if I didn't tweet my aliveness in the next week or so, folks would figure it out. None of my friends or the famous people I've worked with would be releasing a statement about how amazing a person I was, how desperately I'd be missed, and how they couldn't go on living without me. People would see that, clearly, I wasn't gone. I was on TV every week. I didn't have to clear shit up. I just had to be alive. People were commenting "RIP" under all of my photos on Instagram, but I thought it would go away eventually. That it was kind of funny. That it was no big deal. Then my dad called me.

At the time I hadn't spoken to Dad in a little bit under a year. I was working on forgiving him for not being who I needed him to be, but I was in a stage of loving him from afar. He was loving me from afar as well, so when my younger brother Malick showed him what he'd read on Facebook—that I had died of an asthma attack—Dad called me. He said that he'd read something that hurt him very deeply because I was his daughter and he loved me. Somehow we still ended our conversation in a fight. Okay, so maybe I haven't forgiven him completely.

We'll get there. It's complicated. I called my mom after we hung up and told her about the article, the multiplying rumors of my death, and the call from Dad. She laughed and agreed that people will believe anything. We laughed and we laughed and then she must've forgotten all about it.

A week later she called me at eight in the morning and left a message.

"Hi, Gabby. This is Mom. Aunt Mildred just called me and said that she heard on the Internet that you had an asthma attack . . . either last night or this morning . . . and *um* . . . I'm calling to find out if you are okay. Give me a call as soon as you get this message and let me know. Or if anybody is on your phone, please call and let me know what's going on . . . I'll be waiting for your call. Talk to you later."

Aunt Mildred had fallen victim to the same hoax and now so had my mom. Both my parents had called worried that I had died of an asthma attack, and neither of them had considered the fact that I don't actually have asthma. I had to call Mom back as soon as I was awake and remind her that there was a death rumor going around. It wasn't funny anymore. Maybe now was a good time to release a statement.

I went right back to where it all started. Social media. I tweeted again that I was alive. "So many people have tweeted me that I'm dead. Maybe I am. Perhaps my version of hell is people believing poorly written articles about me." That tweet spawned other articles about how the Internet thought I had died but that I was actually alive. A story was created out of something that was never real in the first place. I think that's how journalism works now.

Fuck Twitter yo. I hate Twitter. I love Twitter. I need it to get through a day, but it is also systematically messing with my health and sanity. (At this point in the book, you know how little sanity I actually have left.) I'm constantly on Twitter. I hate the word *twitter*. It's disgusting. It's my best friend. Ugh, FUCK TWITTER! Here's the thing. When Twitter started becoming popular, I refused to join. All of my friends were on it, tweeting away and following celebrity beefs. I thought it was weird that people were tweeting and getting into fights with one another that way. I knew I was missing out on entertaining stuff, but I still thought it was stupid. This one time, I was talking to a rapper (you wouldn't know him) who wanted me to follow him on Twitter so he could follow me back. I said, "Oh, I don't think I'd have anything interesting to say on Twitter. The public doesn't need to know my every single thought. No one is that interesting." The rapper felt insulted and walked away. Whatever. He doesn't get me. Anyway, I just thought that it was kind of vain to think that people want to know everything you're thinking all the time. I could think of maybe two people whose thoughts I'd be open to reading all the time. One guy was a dude I wanted to bone, for obvious reasons (maybe he'd tweet something that would give me clues to help me figure out how to bone him!), and the other guy was my ex-boyfriend, who I wanted to make sure was still terrible so I could constantly give myself a thumbs-up about my decision to break up with him. That's it! Oh! Also Beyoncé. Duh! Other than those three people, I wasn't really interested in Twitter. But lots of my friends thought Twitter was perfect for me. A director I'm close friends with said she was just waiting on me to come around and see that Twitter was the perfect place for my short and sharp wit that would fit nicely into 140 characters. I thought, *True. I am amazing. But what about the people who don't think I'm amazing? Wouldn't they be mean to me on Twitter? I'm sensitive, and I can't really take people being mean to me.* I wasn't convinced Twitter was something I needed in my life.

On the set of *American Horror Story,* I got to work with some amazing actors and actresses. Emphasis on actresses. There were only two men in the cast full-time, so for the bulk of the season, I worked with women. We also hung out together quite a bit. We were constantly around one another. I loved and admired each of those women, but because we are, in fact, women, someone wasn't buying the love. There was a rumor that I was feuding with one of my castmates, Emma Roberts. Reports said that Emma was being a brat on set. That she was rude to everyone and that the cast and crew hated her. The report went on to say that I wasn't having any of that shit so I chewed Emma out in front of everyone and now the two of us were in a fight. But on the brighter side, Emma was being nicer to the crew. This is a story that is 100 percent made-up! First, Emma is lovely. She's also a nerd. She reads books on set. She always has her nose in a book; I don't see how she would find the time to be mean to anyone. Second, I wouldn't yell at someone in front of people. I've been there and it's embarrassing. Third, there were way more interesting things happening on that set than some dumb cat fight, and fourth, I'm super into minding my own damn business. I'm the last one who would say something to someone about the way they act. None of that mattered because the story was more interesting than the truth. It went viral, and people on set started thanking me for getting Emma together. I felt bad that people were thinking that this sweet girl was actually a brat and congratulating me for yelling at her. I decided that I had to do something about it. I had to dispel the rumor.

My Twitter took some time to set up. Like an hour. By the time I was done, I already had two followers. Things were looking up already! But I thought it would be weird if I said to just those two people, "Hey, *um* . . . that thing about me and Emma Roberts is a lie. Just FYI." So I had to gain followers somehow. I told my friends to follow me and they did and they retweeted me, and I had to follow them and then also some celebrities I didn't think would be too annoying to hear from every few minutes. Then I had to post pictures to prove that it was really me, and then I had to read each comment and tweet I received. *American Horror Story* has a huge fan base so the fans were excited to get to talk to me. I still thought this was weird. If I had to be a celebrity in order to be an actor, I preferred to be the kind in a glass tower you couldn't talk to. What was so bad about that? But it turned out that talking to fans was pretty cool. Quickly, Twitter was super fun. I got distracted. Before I knew it, days had gone by and I'd forgotten to dispel the Emma rumor. When I woke up, the first thing I did was check Twitter to see if anyone had been mean to me during the night. (I was always afraid that someone had said something nasty to me right after I fell asleep and that people would see it and agree for eight hours or so before I woke up and could block that person.) Then I checked for who had been nice to me. Then I'd either like that person's tweet or just silently nod my head in agreement: *Yes! I do have great skin.* Then I'd check the verified tab to see if any celebrities had followed me during the night. (I wish the checking didn't fill me with butterflies the way it does, but it does! Leave me alone!)

Then I would get out of bed and go pee. I was hooked on Twitter.

The best part of Twitter is live tweeting. I can live tweet anything! When *American Horror Story* was on every Wednesday night at 10 p.m., my phone was basically glued to my hands. I loved seeing what the fans of the show were saying about it. I couldn't wait to see their tweets about the scariest death scenes or the shocking love scenes that then turned into scary death scenes. It was sort of like being on stage in a play with a rude audience yelling things every few words. Oh! I know! It was just like being a guest on *The Jerry Springer Show*! It was exciting and fascinating to see the audience react in real time.

Eventually I did dispel the rumor that Emma Roberts and I were in a fight. I posted a picture of us together with the caption:

Gabby SidiBae
@GabbySidibe

Emma and I are in a feud?! You sure? #ThatsMyHomeGirl #AintNobodyFuckinwitMyClique

9:19 AM - 4 Nov 2013

See? All good. I wanted to post a caption like "You got beef, Emma? Meet me at the playground at three o'clock and we'll settle this! P.S., Ya momma!" Emma and I would laugh about it, but our followers wouldn't get it.

Twitter is stupid. There are so many truly clever and smart people on Twitter who get the joke and make the joke. They know that Twitter is not to be taken seriously. I'm one of those people. I think Twitter is for saying dumb stuff as soon as it pops into your head. But a ton of my followers don't share my sense of humor. Do you even know how funny I'd be if my followers weren't so sensitive and unfunny? Whenever I post something that makes me laugh, I get a bunch of comments like "That's horrible! You're not better than anyone else! You need to start putting God first! You are so ungrateful!" and I'm all, like, "Chill! I just think it'd be funny if this dog had a mustache." What's equally annoying is when I tell a joke about how terrible a person I am and some of my followers think I really feel that way and tweet their support as if I'm about to jump off the ledge of a building: "Gabby, no! You are a QUEEN! You are seriously the reason I get up out of bed every day! You are so important to me! I love you so much! If I were there with you, I'd hold you in my arms!" That's sweet . . . thanks . . . I was kidding. I realize I'm not really as bad as Hitler because I double-dipped a chip.

What's the solution to a problem like this? I don't think there is a solution. There's hardly a problem. Not everyone in the world shares my sense of humor. That's how the world works. People are different. If we were all the same, we'd all be making out with one another all the time and we'd never get anything done. I understand that some people don't get the joke, so whenever I want to tweet something risky, I make a note of it instead in the notepad of my phone and I keep it. I don't tweet it.

Here's a list of some of my thoughts that were too funny to tweet:

Gabby SidiBae
@GabbySidibe

My New Year's resolution is to start asking Uber drivers to not talk to me without sounding like a bitch . . . fuck it. It's impossible.

(Listen. I wear big-ass headphones over my ears for a reason! I can't hear Beyoncé over your talking about how you got way into gardening and driving around strangers after your youngest left for college in the spring. I mean that's cool and everything, but I'm on my way to the gyno, and I just want to sit here, think my thoughts, and get in formation to receive a stranger's hand in my lady parts. There's no nice way to say this!)

Gabby SidiBae
@GabbySidibe

I wish that money equaled love so that instead of seeing my family I could just give them ten dollars.

(Yo . . . it's becoming harder and harder to actively love people. You have to pay attention to them when they speak and ask follow-up questions. Wouldn't it be nice to just slip your dad twenty bucks instead of discussing the widow he met on eHarmony?)

Gabby SidiBae
@GabbySidibe

I love scenes with Andrea and her grandma cuz they're both the same age. #BeverlyHills90210

(I didn't watch *Beverly Hills 90210* when it was on because I was in elementary school and that's what all the cool girls in my class watched and I was against everything they were into. Turns out, it is a pretty entertaining show, but I'm still glad I waited. Andrea was clearly older than all the other students at that school, but to be fair, they all looked like they were in their early forties. I say that as someone who played a teenager until I was thirty. Also, I never want to tweet something that might hurt someone's feelings and Gabrielle Carteris has always been hella nice to me.)

Gabby SidiBae
@GabbySidibe

It's 6 p.m. and I just remembered that it's Christmas. It's called being a sad lonely adult!

(Christmas is not a time for family when you're a single adult with no kids in your family. What are we doing? Just eating a baked chicken and staring at one another? Fuck outta here. I gotta go be lonely somewhere else. Bye, Mom.)

Gabby SidiBae
@GabbySidibe

I know that babies stare at me cuz they're curious or whatever, but I still kinda want to fight them. #RudeAssBaby

(Your baby is the worst and you know it.)

Gabby SidiBae
@GabbySidibe

I have yet to confirm or deny any love for Adele.

(The weird part about having fans who feel like they could be friends with me is that they want me to like all the same things and people they like. I'm not saying I don't love Adele. I just don't want to confirm it for you so that you can feel close to me. When you sit in your bathtub, crying, eating an entire Entenmann's cake while listening to "Hello," don't call on your image of me to get you through that, baby girl. Take that time for yourself. I'll be waiting for you to talk about happy things when you're done.)

Gabby SidiBae
@GabbySidibe
Seriously! What the fuck is James Franco's deal?! I'm sick of it, James! SICK OF IT!

(I don't think I need to explain this to you. Fucking James Franco thinks he can do anything!)

Gabby SidiBae
@GabbySidibe
Oprah is being completely unrealistic about Weight Watchers. Counting points is not a game. THIS IS MY LIFE, OPRAH!!!

(There's nothing I find funnier than Oprah. Oprah is the greatest gift God has given to this world. By "God" I mean "Oprah," of course. Oprah has given us the gift of Oprah. Praise Oprah. May Oprah be with you.)

Gabby SidiBae
@GabbySidibe
I say the phrase "You Bitch! I'll kill you! I'll murder your whole

family!" entirely too much even though I'm laughing when I'm saying it. I just know it's gonna bite me in the ass one day.

(Truly, I should stop threatening to kill people when I don't really mean it. That's what got O. J. Simpson caught up. Of course I'm kidding again; O. J. did it . . . allegedly . . . obviously . . . I mean allegedly.)

Gabby SidiBae
@GabbySidibe

Look. I don't care for dinosaurs. If I can't ride one, what do I care what lived billions of years ago? You didn't even know it had feathers until like three years ago! Mind ya business, stupid!

(Look, I know I'm in the minority here, but I really hate dinosaurs. I hate them. Maybe hating them is how I process my fear that one day they'll come back somehow. I couldn't sit through *Jurassic Park*. I'm so grateful that we don't have to live beside those giant monsters. But how can we be sure that some evil scientist with plans to rule the world won't bring dinosaurs back into existence? What will we do then, society?!)

Gabby SidiBae
@GabbySidibe

I'm starting to think that the only way I can lose weight is by running over an old Gypsy woman with my car so that her dad can put a curse on me. I'll gladly take that curse even if I didn't get to hit someone with my car for it!

(I was watching that Stephen King movie *Thinner*, including its questionable Gypsy-woman scene, and thought, *Shit*

. . . this lawyer's starting to look really good, but then it went too far.)

Gabby SidiBae
@GabbySidibe
Keep tweeting me to ask if I'm alive and I'll prove that I'm alive by blocking people dumb enough to tweet me to see if I'm alive. #TestMe

(I might actually tweet this before this day is over.)

There! You read them and you're still alive! It wasn't that bad! What's great is that I have plenty of followers who do get my jokes and think I'm funny. Clearly, those people are my favorites. Plenty of people hate me, though. Plenty of people tweet me to hurt my feelings, and I used to get really upset about it. I would start angrily typing out a response to them and then I'd think, *No! That's what they want you to do!* That person wants my attention. My attention will tell them that they exist and that they matter to me. If I say nothing, they'll stay a ghost and have to float on to find someone else to verify their existence. But most times I still really want to respond. So I block the mean commenters. I disable myself from answering them. Sure, a lot of people take pride in being blocked. They see that I have noticed them, but that's okay. I don't have to see them rejoicing in whatever they get from having me block them. Honestly, I block people all the time. And I'll admit, I do it for small, petty reasons. I block people who are mean to me, to my friends, or to my other followers. I block people who nastily tell me to lose weight. I block people who tell me that they love me but that they want to see me lose weight and live a healthier life. Those people have no idea how hard I'm fighting for my life every day of it. I block people who say they don't like my outfits. I block people who don't like my hair. I block people who tweet that they don't like my blonde hair on *Empire*. Hi! *Empire* is a TV show! I didn't get to choose my character's hair color, but it's my job to wear it. I can't do anything about it. You can do even less about it cuz ya blocked! Oh! You think I shouldn't wear red? I LOVE wearing red! Don't worry. You won't see me wear red cuz YA BLOCKED! Okay, honestly, I could probably chill and take a step back to keep my blocking finger from being so itchy. I'm aware that I run my social-media pages like Stalin. But I'm very sensitive, and at the same time (like Stalin), I've ended up with a job and a life that means I have followers. It's weird, but I do. I don't control much, but I control what I can. I prefer for my world to smell like strawberries and look like rainbows, and at least on Twitter I can block negative comments, fighting, and opinions about what I should be doing in my life. I am compulsive about keeping those dark clouds out of my world. Choose your tweets wisely.

P.S.: When I *do* die, don't let Lifetime do a movie about my life.

10

GABOUREY, BUT YOU CAN CALL ME GABBY

The world's gonna know your name.
What's your name, man?

— Aaron Burr (*Hamilton*)

BACK WHEN I WAS WAITING for my real life as an actress and all-around dope celebrity to start, I would wake up every day to do nothing but wait for Lee Daniels to call me. He called to tell me huge news like when *Push* (as *Precious* was still called then) was submitted to the Sundance Film Festival for its debut. Sometimes he'd call to give practical advice like what I should wear to the premiere and for interviews. He'd tell me that I should start watching Halle Berry in her interviews so I could emulate her. She was ladylike and I, apparently, was not. I promised I would watch her, but I knew I was lying when I said it. Again, I'm not polite enough to pretend to be someone else for long. Other times he'd just call to fanta-

size with me about what life would be like after the movie was
released officially.

"Gabbala! Are you ready? Are you ready!? Your life is going
to be completely different! What are you going to do?"

"What am I going to do about what?" I'd ask.

"What are you going to do when people come up to you in
the street, and say, 'Precious, you changed my life.'"

"What? No one's gonna do that!" I was sure of it.

"Yes, they will! They will come right up to you and tell you
about all of the pain and abuse they've suffered the way Precious has. A lot of people will identify with her and will identify with you. What are you going to say to people who see
themselves in Precious and in you?"

"That's crazy!" I was beginning to feel nauseated. Maybe I
should figure out how Halle Berry deals with that.

"Get ready, Gabby. You're going to be more than just a regular person now. You're going to be Precious."

"Well . . . shit . . . I hadn't thought of it. I guess I'll start by
saying, 'My name is Gabby.'"

"You can't say that! Your name is Precious now!" he ex-
claimed.

"What? Is that rude? Cuz . . . I really love my name."

"Well, get ready, bitch!" Lee said, laughing.

My relationship with my name is a serious one. I love my
name. "Gabourey," with its pretty little three-syllable melody
and its French accent, has always sounded like a song to me.
A flower. A perfume. A bridge. A chemical element found in
the ground, in a cave, in Africa, at the birth of civilization. My

name is special. It is my first gift from my father. Something
he gave me.

Months after the premiere of *Push* at Sundance, and after
Oprah and Tyler Perry joined our film, I finally got it: I was
about to lose my name. At Sundance, people who saw the film
really thought that Precious was my first name. Regular people, members of the media, and filmmakers alike were all surprised to find out that my name wasn't actually Precious and
that I was an actor. Really smart people! I was heartbroken
when Lee called me to tell me that they had decided to change
the name of the film from *Push* to *Precious: Based on the Novel
"Push" by Sapphire*. First, could the title be any longer? Second, I was sure that anyone who heard the title without knowing what the movie was about would assume it was a chick
flick and wouldn't be interested. *Precious*? For lack of a better
word, it sounded too . . . precious. Was it the story about a cartoon puppy on a quest to find its favorite chew toy? A girl who
falls in love and cries a bunch? That's not interesting! Third, I
knew that while this days-long title might be the official one
the unofficial and most used title for the film, my first, would
be *Precious*. I would now be synonymous with this word and
this name forever. I'd be her name, her story. I figured that
some people would understand I had a self and a name aside
from Precious, but I knew that once they heard my African-
ass name with its six syllables and accents, they'd prefer to go
back to calling me Precious. Why? Because Americans are lazy.
They're also kind. Also condescending. They can't pronounce
my name, Gabourey, but don't want to try in case they get
it wrong and hurt my feelings, so they decide that my name
is Gabby, something their lazy tongues *can* pronounce. I, as

a person with a hard-to-pronounce name, should be understanding and chill about it. I should allow people to be comfortable calling me something other than my name. It's the polite thing to do. Unfortunately for lazy people, I am impolite. I am an asshole, and my name is Gabourey Sidibe.

Dad named me Gabourey MaLingair Sidibe. I just found out that *Gabourey* means "the one with the beautiful cheeks." Like, duh. Have you even SEEN my cheeks? All plump and round. You just want to bite them! My face ain't half bad, either. *MaLingair* is actually two words that in Wolof mean "my queen." All of Dad's children have Senegalese names because all of his children are Senegalese. I am his second child and his first daughter. My name is a *turendo,* a word that in Wolof means namesake. I was named decades before my birth. Before Dad's marriage to Mom and before he was even a grown man. My name is and has been Gabourey since his childhood; it's the delivery of a promise Dad made to a woman who loved and helped to raise him. Gabouré.

I knew that Dad had an older sister from his father's previous marriage to a woman who died during childbirth. His father was often gone, busy with politics and his other families. Much like Dad, my grandfather had several wives and families to attend to, just like the average Senegalese man. Dad was left to help his mother and watch over his younger siblings. I remember my grandparents very well as they died when I was in my early twenties, but I realized I knew very little about Gabouré.

"She's ninety years old now!" Dad told me. "She uses a cane now. She asked me about you. She always wants to see you."

"She's your aunt or something, right?"

"Ahh, no. Not my aunt, but she took care of me like I was her child."

"Why?" I asked.

"Well . . . Maybe I shouldn't say."

Already this call was better than I had anticipated. Most things about Dad's early life in Senegal he'd never shared with me. Maybe it's because I was young or a girl. Or I wasn't smart enough to ask aloud instead of wondering in silence who this man was.

"I shouldn't say, but I was an abused child," he continued. I listened quietly, the idea of Dad being a child at all—not so much the part about the abuse—blowing my mind.

"My father didn't talk to us. He only talked about politics and we were children. My mother was very cold to me. She was a mean lady, so Gabouré took me in and cared for me." I was now clearing my throat so that I wouldn't sound like I was crying.

"Did you live with her?"

"No. I didn't live with her. She lived in the neighborhood and she had kids and I would go to her house and she would feed me and take care of me and love me. She loved me like my mother didn't. She was so kind to me and I said to her, 'If I have a daughter, I will name her after you.' She was so happy to hear that. Her sons, her family, everyone was so happy to hear that I wanted to name you after her, and when I grew up, I kept my promise. So! You are my daughter, Gabourey, after that lady I loved and who loved me so much. She took care of me when my own mother didn't like me. I see her when I go back and she always asks about you."

• • •

Dad is the first man I fell in love with and the first man I fell out of love with. Before I was done with him, he was my hero. He knew a little bit about almost everything. He spoke French and he drank tea. Somehow, while hardly ever smiling or laughing, he introduced me to comedy. I would watch *The Benny Hill Show* with him and see what made him and other people like him laugh. People on the other side of the world in Africa and Europe. People who weren't like Mom and Ahmed and me. We were new people, but Africans were the first people, according to Dad. The rest of the world was young by comparison. America especially. Everything Dad did seemed fancy and correct.

Dad would sit me on his chest and tell me the way my grown-up life would be, and I'd love his attention but hate every word of his marriage-to-a-nice-Muslim-man plans for me. I was too American! He'd also draw beautiful houses for me in pen and tell me that one day he'd build that house for me to live in. Huts on the beach with blue-ink palm trees in the front yard. Stately mansions with a Rolls-Royce parked in the garage, drawn in black ink. I'd ask if I could color it in, and he'd say, "Of course! It's your house!" When I was upset, he'd take my chin in his hand, and say, "What's wrong with my princess, huh? My queen! What happened to my baby? Who did it?" I would frown harder to make my face look as pitiful as possible and lodge whatever complaint I had, and he'd say, "Come on! You're a big girl now. You're so pretty, my queen. All the time sad, that's no good! Why you don't smile?" "I HATE smiling!" I would answer back, and he'd laugh, and say, "You trying to hurt your daddy?" Then I'd feel horrible and hug him and start crying.

I loved the entire FUCK out of Dad. I loved Mom, too, and she was hella fun and everything, don't get me wrong, but Dad had a bigger payoff for me. Getting him to laugh felt like a big accomplishment. I would ask him questions ad nauseam that he wouldn't answer, and he would tell me that I was too smart for my own good, which I took as a compliment. I would insist that he would be much more handsome if he shaved his face. We would argue, and he'd say, "You just like your mammy! All the time talking!" Every now and then he would shave his ever-present mustache to satisfy me. He was right and I was wrong about it, but I would never admit that to him. I was too high on the power I held over his face. He was a better cook than Mom, and he'd let me help him in the kitchen. He'd tell me that he was teaching me to be a wife, and I guess I used to be down with that shit because I would stand on a chair in our tiny kitchen and watch everything he did. The best thing about my father was that when it came to my social coping skills he let me be me. Mom would try to teach me to use my words instead of my fists, but Dad would laugh every time I told him about beating up some boy in my class who had disrespected me. Dad liked that I was tough, so I liked that I was tough. I was Rocky and he was my Mickey. Mom would say, "You're so mean, just like ya daddy." She meant to shame me I'm sure, but it made me proud instead. I wasn't mean. I was tough. Dad and I were Africans who had to live in America. We had African faces. African skin color. And we both had African names. My dad knew what it was to be different when everyone around you is the same.

I was Gabourey M. Sidibe in American elementary school, in a pre–*Lion King* world. I was Gabourey in a school of Jennifers, Stacies, Ericas, and Elizabeths. Brandons, Johnnies, and Anthonies. My round little belly and my dark chocolate skin made me look different, and the way I singsonged my African name made me sound different. Teachers would always mispronounce my name.

"Gab . . . Gob . . . GaborNay Sid . . . Side-Bee?"

"Gabourey Sidibe." I'd probably say it with an eye roll.

"That's pretty! What is it?"

"It's African."

"Oh! Where were you born?"

"Brooklyn."

" . . ."

"My dad's from Senegal."

"What's that?"

"It's a country in Africa."

"Oh! Can we call you Gabby?"

"No. My name is Gabourey. It rhymes with *cabaret*."

Everyone agreed that my name was pretty, but they also agreed that ain't nobody got time to say it. I hated being called Gabby when I was in elementary school. It made my skin crawl. Mom had tried to nickname me Gabby when I was a baby, but legend has it that I refused to respond to it. I knew who I was, and letting others call me Gabby meant letting them call me by someone else's name. I would not give that convenience to the kids and teachers in my school. They called me Gabby anyway. I just wouldn't respond. I'd respond to all the other names they called me. Fatty, Pig, Black Pig, Hog, African Booty Scratcher. I usually responded with my fists. Later, I responded with tears and panic attacks on top of my fists. (Real quick, African Booty Scratcher is probably the most specific and regional insult ever. As if Europeans, Americans, and Asians don't scratch their booties. Booties itch no matter where you come from! Logistically, that insult just doesn't work. The other names were way better insults.)

It wasn't until junior high school that I changed my mind about Gabby. Listen, I knew I was intense. I was a hard-core kid on purpose, and it left me lonely, reading books at lunch, and going straight home from school by myself every day. I knew I had to change my attitude about a lot of things in junior high. For some reason, junior high school kids seemed at least five years older than the kids who'd just graduated from elementary school a few months ago. I had to grow up fast! Also, I was now in a class with kids who didn't know what an intense creep I was. It was a fresh start, and I could be anyone I wanted to be. Gabourey had failed at making friends in elementary, so I figured it was time to give Gabby a try. As long as it was my decision to allow people to call me that. I am stubborn that way. Gabby was certainly easier to say and apparently easier to deal with. She was friendlier and joked around a lot more than Gabourey. Gabourey was way serious and Gabby was not. Gabourey was like one of those super-expensive Barbies that you have to buy at FAO Schwarz, and Gabby was a Cabbage Patch doll that your aunt's weird friend might give you because her ex-boyfriend's daughter left it at her house and she just wants it gone. I was still Gabourey at home; I reserved Gabby for school and the outside world. Gabby wasn't and still isn't my name. Gabby is more like a character I play. Maybe that's too complicated?

I've been to Senegal—where people can pronounce my

name—with Dad and Ahmed more times than I actually remember. My first trip there, I was a baby in diapers. My only
memory of that visit was finding a can of coffee and mistak-
ing it for chocolate. It tasted horrible, but I kept eating, thinking that maybe after the fifth handful it would be delicious. My
dumb little toddler body eventually shat coffee out of nearly
every orifice. That's not an easy memory to forget. But my
memories of my last visit to Senegal are the reason I have
vowed never to go back.

The summer I turned seven, Dad, Ahmed, and I flew to Senegal with two huge suitcases to see Dad's family. Mom stayed
home. I remember how excited everyone was to see Dad. I
thought maybe he was secretly famous in Senegal in a way
that he wasn't in Brooklyn. All of Dad's younger brothers admired him. Asin was my favorite Senegalese uncle. He was almost as handsome as Dad. He smoked cigarettes and rode a
motorcycle. He was what I thought my dad would be if he
hadn't had kids. Dad had a bunch of girlie sisters who loved
to dress me up in traditional African dresses and braid my
hair. They'd teach dances to Ahmed and me, and laugh and
clap their hands while we danced for them. All day long Dad's
mom would make *bissap* icies and sell them out of the house
to neighborhood kids. She looked a lot like my mom, as we
know, and loved to hug Ahmed and me and test our Wolof. My
grandfather was basically the most superior human I'd ever
met. He was like King Jaffe Joffer in *Coming to America*. He was
a tall man with a big laugh. He took all of his meals in his bedroom while everyone else ate together with their hands out of
two huge bowls in the kitchen. A bowl for the girls and a bowl

for the boys. Grandpa would let us eat with him in his bed. He had a plate and a fork. He was the only man in the world who was the boss of Dad.

The first two weeks of this trip to Senegal were magical. Dad, Asin, and Grandpa took us to Gorée Island to the beach. It was a tourist attraction by then, but Gorée Island started out as a port for the slave trade to America and Europe. We went to the "bush" in Thiès to visit family living on a farm with animals. We took a train to see Saint-Louis (Senegal has its own Saint Louis!!!), and it looked just like New Orleans. We met and played with gorgeous chocolate- and charcoal-skinned kids just like us who played games with us that didn't require words. Dad took us to shopping malls and food markets, where I ate some of the best things I've ever tasted. Foods I still remember to this day. Let me really quickly put you up on game. Chocolate in Senegal is THE BEST! And when you heat it up and slather it on a fresh baguette . . . holy shit!! It's like a chocolate croissant but somehow better! Get outta here! It's so fucking good! Everyone wanted to see Dad and his American children with African names, so we went to the homes of a lot of his friends and family and people would always cook delicious meals for us.

But then Dad left. He had planned to stay in Senegal for two weeks and then leave Ahmed and me there for the rest of the summer so that we could get to know his family.

Dad's family went from being welcoming to being monsters. His mother turned cold and cruel to us. She let Dad's younger brothers hit us. The girls weren't any nicer, and the dancing became more mandatory than recreational. They called me Patapoof, which is Wolof for "fat," and called us both Americans in a snotty way, making it clear that it was an insult. If Mom sent us a care package, we'd have very little time to play with anything before it was gone. If Mom and Dad called us to see how we were doing, someone would stand by us to make sure we weren't telling. It was horrible. We were seven and eight years old with no real sense of time and no way of knowing if we were ever going to go home. Our parents knew what the plan was — they planned to book a standby flight for the two of us to come home — but Ahmed and I were basically in the dark and just trying to survive. Several times we were driven to the airport thinking we were going home only to be driven right back to Dad's family.

My grandpa was still hella dope to us! The others wouldn't hurt us around him. Problem is, he was gone a lot visiting his other families. We never knew when he was coming back. Asin was still nice to us, but he was also gone a lot. He had lots of friends and probably a lot of girls. Ahmed and I found it better to be out of the house. We made friends in the neighborhood and would find solace at the homes of those friends. Much like Dad had learned to do when he found Gabouré.

When we finally left Senegal, we each had a backpack. Whatever was in those two huge suitcases when we arrived belonged to the bush now. We told Mom and Dad what we had endured, and they were very upset. Mom even threw up. This is when I vowed never to step foot in Senegal again. I was pissed. I meant it. I stopped speaking Wolof to Dad when he would speak it to me. I didn't want to be Senegalese anymore. I decided I would rather be named Lisa Simpson than Gabourey Sidibe. That didn't last too long. Honestly, the feeling of superiority I got from being "foreign" even though I really wasn't was too powerful. Every one of our American family members wanted to know all about our time in Senegal. All of my teachers at school wanted to know what Africa was like. It gave me an edge. I knew something they didn't. And not just the obvious, like how there actually weren't lions roaming the streets, but also all the beautiful things I got to experience there, like the food, culture, clothes, music, and people — the ones outside my own family. I realized that I didn't hate Senegal. I hated the Sidibes.

Still, I said I'd never go back to Senegal and I meant it. I've gone to South Africa on safari and ate delicious food and did much more. But it wasn't Senegal. It wasn't home. Dad has offered to take me with him to Senegal over and over again. I always decline. "I have my own home there! No one's gonna bother you!" he says. I just shake my head. "We'll buy your return ticket so that you know when you are leaving. I won't make you fly standby!" "Nah fam," I respond. Why? Because I'm an idiot. I made up my mind when I was seven and stuck to it.

That ends here. I'm not a helpless child anymore. I'm a grown-up and I have my own money. I can stay where I want. I just realized that never stepping foot in Senegal is the same as letting a seven-year-old tell me what to do. Fuck outta here. I choose to make up my own grown-up mind about Senegal, and about Dad.

"Dad, am I anything like Gabouré?"

"Oh, yes! Very much so. She is very outgoing like you. She is very smart and outspoken. Very smart. She's very talkative. Everybody likes her." It's so strange to know that in spite of my being a monster asshole to him over the years he still thinks of me in this way. I'm still good enough to carry the African name of the woman who saved him.

As of right now, I plan to go back to Senegal with Dad so I can experience him and his country as an adult. Maybe I'll even be open to meeting his other little princesses . . . to let them know that I am the queen!

11

MYOB: MIND YOUR OWN BODY

I feel really annoyed right now ... I should
eat a few cookies.

— me ... like all the fucking time!

GUESS I WAS AROUND six years old when I started to notice that I was a fat kid. Maybe *notice* is a strong word. I was
in my body, so I didn't spend a lot of time looking at it yet. I
just took in that people said things about me that they didn't
say about other kids. I didn't really get why other kids called
me fatso or elephant, or why they felt they could talk about my
body at all. My mom was fat. Most of her family was as well.
My dad was thin but had a pretty big stomach that he blamed
on American food. I thought I looked like my family, and that
seemed right and fine with me. Also, it was hard to imagine
that there was something wrong with my body when I knew
that it was temporary. That's what little kids do. They grow.
Their bodies change.

Eventually, I noticed my own family starting to talk about my weight. I used to do this thing when I was in kindergarten. At the end of school, I would see my mom and run as fast as I could and plow into her for a hug. She would hug me back, and say, "Ugh! Gabu! You're like a football player. You're gonna knock me over." I took this as a challenge, and every day I would try to plow into her harder because I thought it was a fun ritual we had. One day she told me that I was hurting her because I was too big. I remember that I didn't get it at first and continued to do this to her for who knows how much longer. But then my brother started calling me fatso, hippo, and the names of many other large animals, like the kids at school did, and I started calling him an idiot and stupid on a daily basis as well. Siblings, right? I still didn't really notice there was a problem until my father started suggesting that I lose weight so that he could show everyone what a pretty princess he had for a daughter. That's when I realized that I was different from other kids, and that this affected the people around me. It had never occurred to me that I looked bad in a way that would make my father not want his friends to know he had a daughter. It took so long to realize that my body was different, but it took about two seconds to jump to that conclusion.

My mom said that when I was a baby I wouldn't eat anything and stayed underweight. My doctor told her to put a few iron drops in my food. She says she put in the recommended amount and that it worked—too well—I haven't stopped eating yet. Every time she tells me this story now, I'm like, "TRUE!" because this is, after all, a story of triumph. My mother also told me that her family blamed her for my weight. I thought it was completely unfair of her family—I knew that

I was the one who ate too much. I was the one who really liked cookies and cakes and ice cream. It was one thing to bring shame to my dad, but my mom was wonderful and she could do no wrong. I was so mad at her family for making her feel bad about something she wasn't in control of, and I felt terrible for being something wrong in her life.

When my parents separated, my mom started giving me diet pills. The purpose of diet pills is to suppress your appetite. But I'd learned that you can actually eat when you're *not* hungry. Eating had nothing to do with appetite anymore. If I had a bad day at school, munching Chips Ahoy! cookies while watching cartoons was a great way to elevate my mood! If someone hurt my feelings by calling me fat, an excellent way to stop feeling hurt was to eat a bowl of Neapolitan ice cream! If I had a good day and everything was fine, that called for a celebration of both ice cream *and* cookies! I was now self-soothing and also rewarding myself with food. If I ever had a free moment with nothing fun to do, like do you even *know* how fun BBQ Pringles can be? Fun enough to stomp out the boredom! Eating had nothing to do with appetite, so those pills didn't work.

The first year my parents separated, Ahmed and I went to live with my dad in Brooklyn for the summer. Ahmed wasn't thin, but he was thinner than I was and often went outside to play football with his friends in the heat. He lost weight all summer long while I sat friendless in the house all day. Right before summer started, I'd accidentally shot myself in the foot while playing with a Roman candle on the stoop in front of my aunt Dorothy's house and suffered a third-degree burn. I had to have my bandage changed every other day all summer. I watched TV all day long and ate all day long, too. Dad bought me SlimFast shakes to help me lose weight. I drank the shakes along with some chips while watching TV and feeling sorry for myself. That same summer, Dad took Ahmed to Senegal and France to visit family. He left me in Brooklyn with Tola and the new baby, Abdul. I don't remember ever voicing this, but I thought he'd taken Ahmed and not me because he was ashamed of me. In all likelihood, he had enough money to take only one kid, and Ahmed was easier than I was. I asked too many questions and by then I'd already declared that I hated Senegal and never wanted to go back. Also, I had a steak-size hole in my foot. I'm sure Ibnou's reasons had nothing to do with my weight, but I still thought I was too big for him to want to admit that he was my father.

That was the summer my panic attacks started. I remember crying and complaining that I couldn't breathe. It's easy to see now that with my parents' separation, my new step-mom and brother, moving into my aunt Dorothy's house, my fireworks accident, the antibiotics I had to take for my foot—along with the diet pills—life was out of control for me. At the same time, I had two parents whose lives had also changed dramatically. I don't think they noticed what was happening to me. I was nine years old and my family was split in two and I was too fat for either family. Everything hurt and it hurt too deeply. I was all of a sudden really sensitive; if someone called me a name, I'd cry for hours. That fall, Ahmed and I went back to living with Mom and never tried that "summers with Dad" experiment again. Thank God. If I was going to be too fat for my family, I preferred to be with the parent who was also fat. Mom. Before their split, Dad was diagnosed with diabetes, and he immediately changed his eating habits and lost his big stomach. All of a sudden, he became rail thin with very little effort. I was so jealous. Mom had been a fat little girl like me, and I figured she understood me. Problem is, she was also a fat grown-up, and she didn't want me eventually to be the same. Some days she called me names just as hurtful as the ones the kids in school used. She thought she was helping me. I'm sure she knew that she was making me hate her, too, but I think she probably thought it would be worth it if I lost weight. But I didn't. I just hated her.

She tried to help in positive ways, too. Mom signed Ahmed and me up for swim classes near Aunt Dorothy's house. Two days a week, we went to class and then walked home. I started to lose weight, but swim classes were soon over. Next, Mom enrolled me in dance class. That helped for a while, too, but when classes ended, the weight came back again. My diet never changed. It was whatever Mom cooked or whatever she'd bring home after singing in the subway. Burgers, Chinese food, pizza, whatever. There were usually Oreo cookies and ice cream around because that's what my mom liked to eat. Shit. Me, too. She'd yell at me not to eat those things, but the yelling paled compared to the satisfaction I got from eating the Oreos. Also, fuck outta here! Maybe if the house was filled with salad.

In junior high the panic attacks became an everyday occurrence. Children who were sweet little kids the year before become monsters in junior high who make fun of you relentlessly until you cry. And when you cry, they make fun of you for crying. There is no escape. Even your best friends hate you. And you hate them just as much. You only hang out with them because junior high is easier in packs, but it's still horrible. Not only do kids not give a fuck about your feelings, they actually *want* to hurt you. My junior high was like a Vietnamese minefield. I would pray every day that God would make me less sensitive. I knew that no matter what someone was going to make fun of me every day, and I prayed to be able to hold my tears. The boys I had crushes on would call me a cheeseburger (now that I think of it, I don't know why being called a cheeseburger hurt me so badly, but it was like a knife to the heart when I was twelve). Junior high is where I learned that if I couldn't stop the jokes about my weight I could make them first. Like exaggerating my weight was part of some elaborate comedy act. If we were in phys ed and made to run around the gym a few times, I knew I'd be slow. So I'd make a big deal of how tired I was and how crazy it was that anyone would believe that I could "drag my fat ass around a gym." My classmates would laugh and root me on as I loudly yelled, "Oh, GOD! I'm not gonna make it! I'm just gonna lay down and die!" while slowly jogging around the room. This way, at least I didn't cry, and my fellow junior high psychopaths laughed and wanted to be around me. Sure, they were partly laughing *at* me, but the joke was on my terms so they were also laughing *with* me. I think. I had friends in junior high. Plenty of friends. Most of them continued to hurt my feelings one way or another, though. I would try to hurt their feelings, too. I don't feel comfortable saying that I was a victim of bullying. Yes, I was bullied, but I was also the bully. Some of the worst, most regrettable things I've ever done in my life, I did in junior high. Junior high is a battleground. It's as if every day there's so much shit weighing on you that you have to find someone weaker to dump it all on. As horrible as it was, I had the greatest time in junior high. I just kinda wanted to die every day, too.

High school wasn't much different than junior high except there were even more cute boys who pretended to like me only to laugh in my face when I looked hopeful. By now I realized that my parents, Mom especially, held more responsibility for my weight than they ever claimed. It wasn't all her fault, but it certainly wasn't all mine, either. I didn't cook for myself or buy groceries. I didn't bring cookies and ice cream into the house. I didn't know salad could be something other than my mom's version: iceberg lettuce with ketchup-and-mayonnaise dressing slathered on every piece. (We'd all feel smug and satisfied with ourselves for eating that version of a salad, and then we wouldn't do it again for like a year.) Oddly enough, as soon as I realized that my weight wasn't entirely my fault, it became my responsibility from that moment on. I figured I could do better. Now I was always making meal plans with my friends. Trying new diets where I would only eat packs of ramen noodles and only drink Crystal Light. The women in the commercials for Crystal Light all looked so pretty, skinny, and happy. And the word *light* was in the title! Obviously, it was better for me than Kool-Aid. Those diets never lasted long because McDonald's and soda felt better and the most consistent food in our house was still takeout.

During high school, I stopped eating lunch. I never ate breakfast to begin with, and now I gave up lunch completely, too. There were no nutritionists around to tell me that it's counterproductive *not* to eat, so it felt like the healthy thing to do. It wasn't just because school lunch was horrible and there were mice running around our lunchroom. (Literally! The local news came to do a story on how terrible my school's lunch was. They even interviewed ME! My first-ever interview!) I stopped eating lunch because I couldn't help thinking that people were watching me eat and were disgusted by me because I was fat. I just stopped. Hungry or not, I wouldn't eat until I was home from school, whether it was at 3 p.m. or 10 p.m.

Exercising was out of the question during high school for several reasons. Swim class was long over. Also I was super lazy. Going to gym class was wildly inconvenient. It was the last period of my day on the tenth floor; most of my classes were on the fifth floor. Walking up five flights and changing clothes in a locker room full of high school bitches just to get picked last to play volleyball didn't seem worth it. My senior year I had to take gym at night school and write an independent study on sports in order to graduate. Night-school gym class was from seven to nine-thirty twice a week in the basement of my high school. The final exam consisted of one hundred push-ups and three hundred jumping jacks. Every class got us closer to that final—if I didn't pass it, I wouldn't graduate. I couldn't afford to be lazy. I started dropping weight fast. I'd get home starving at eleven at night, quickly eat dinner, and then go to bed just as quickly and get up the next day in time for eight o'clock class. It felt like finally someone was putting their foot down and making exercise a priority for me, and it was the New York City Public Schools. I lost a lot of weight; I graduated.

I'd survived childhood, but the weight was back on in a matter of weeks.

• • •

The other night I was at dinner with a friend, a woman eleven years older than I am but who looks my age and is gorgeous. She's got shiny dark hair, olive skin, a beautiful face, a nice rack, and a small waist. She's also hella smart and funny, for all you men out there reading this and wondering, *But what about her* personality!? While I've been friends with her for a few years, and we've gone out to dinner and lunch numerous times, we don't know everything about each other. I was very surprised when the two of us began reminiscing about our eating disorders like two veterans of a secret war. We were fondly recalling times when we would sneak off to the bathroom during a night out with friends to throw up on purpose. We both rolled our eyes at the thought; if we did such a thing today, our friends would instantly know what's up so . . . we'd better not try it anymore.

It was nice talking to my friend about my eating disorder. I'd never really talked about it in this way before to anyone. I usually mention it, if I bring it up at all, as something terrible that I survived. That's all most of my friends can accept. But my eating disorder was more like an abusive boyfriend. It was harmful, but it could be really sweet sometimes. It was hard to break up with because I loved it. I've never admitted to anyone how much I miss it. How much good it brought me even though it was constantly kicking my ass. Barrassing.

Yep! If you're keeping score, add an eating disorder to the growing list of cute and quirky facts about me. Panic attacks, unhealthy eating habits, and bulimia. Soooo *cute!* The bulimia started in my second year at college and stuck around for about three years. It took a lot of therapy to figure out why I was doing it and then how to stop. Even though it's been years since I was in the thick of that behavior, I still struggle with figuring out how to stop thinking about throwing up after I eat.

Even though—duh!—throwing up can cause so many problems. Stomach acid can give you sores in your mouth and burn the lining of your esophagus. Throwing up dehydrates you and can cause a host of cardiovascular problems. It's dangerous. Also, HELLO! Vomit is nasty! It's liquefied food that will soon be shit. LITERALLY! It makes your breath smell, your eyes bulge, and your throat burns like hell so you cough every few minutes. Also, your friends know. You think you're fooling them, but you're not.

Before I even knew I was having panic attacks, I'd start crying about whatever and be unable to stop. I mean really! I'd spend hours crying if some dude I liked was rude to me. Or if my best friend and I had plans but then she canceled to stay home and write her term paper. My emotions were out of control, and all I could do was cry about it for hours in my room. One day I cried so hard and long that I started vomiting. When I was done, I wasn't crying anymore. I wasn't even thinking about what had made me cry to begin with. I felt empty, which was a great thing—before this, I'd felt too full of emotions. It was like pushing a reset button. The next time I couldn't stop crying, a lightbulb went off in my head, and I ran to the bathroom and jammed my finger down my throat. It made me feel high. It was a little like that happiness you get from the endorphins that are triggered when you work out. I felt a release around my head like a halo that made me feel lighter psychically and emotionally. I'd found a new way to deal with the emotions I was drowning in.

Because I was depressed, I had no appetite, so on days when

I couldn't stop crying and needed to throw up even though I had an empty stomach, I would eat a slice of bread, drink a bottle of water, and then immediately throw that up. I wasn't even trying to lose weight—that's not the way it works. I was trying to stop myself from crying, and throwing up made me feel like I had some magic trick to keep my negative emotions at bay.

After I got some therapy and figured out how to deal with most of my emotions while keeping my fingers away from my throat, I turned my attention to actually *trying* to lose weight. I figured that since I was becoming mentally healthy I should focus on becoming physically healthy as well. At the age of twenty-two, when I hadn't purposely thrown up or starved myself for six months, I made an appointment with a bariatric surgeon to discuss having weight-loss surgery. Part of that process is a psychological evaluation. I had to see a therapist, not my own, who would determine if I was mentally capable of having the surgery. Surprise! I wasn't. The therapist said that because I had just battled an eating disorder I needed much more time to heal from it before I got surgery. When people get weight-loss surgery, their stomachs are reduced to the size of an egg. Overweight people usually continue to overeat, and when that happens on a stomach the size of an egg, you throw up. For someone like me who enjoyed throwing up, the surgery was too risky. The therapist suggested that I give it a year or two before having another psychological evaluation. I had screwed myself out of the surgery. I started throwing up again later that night; quitting is for quitters. Luckily, I didn't have to do it for three more years. I was able to break the habit.

• ● •

When I got my first film role, no one was more surprised than I was. I did take pleasure in the fact that someone had hired me to star in a real live movie. And I was clear that I wouldn't have gotten the role if I was skinny. Precious was a role for fat girls only! What a weird world we live in, huh? Lee Daniels said he wanted me to be a star even after *Precious*; he wanted me to be able to endure the grueling pace of making movies. He immediately signed me up for a gym, hired me a personal trainer, put me in tap-dancing class, and hired a yoga instructor for me. He wanted me to be moving six days a week, and I did. I didn't complain at all! I was ecstatic that someone was taking charge of my body in this healthy way and, on top of that, paying for it! All I had to do was *not* eat like an asshole, and that was pretty easy when being a movie star was going to depend on it. I was up every morning at six. I would kind of eat breakfast and then go to the gym to work out with my trainer. Then I'd rehearse with Lee, and then he'd drive me to the production office where Lee's staff would order me a healthy lunch. I'd do some fittings for clothes, sign some paperwork, have a meeting, and then I'd go to tap-dance class for two or three hours and then home to make myself a healthy dinner, and I did it all again the next day. On the weekends I'd go to yoga. I lost nearly thirty pounds in the first month of this, and for the first time, the only thing I gained was a strong hate for yoga. Fuck yoga yo.

I continued to lose weight as we filmed. When we were done, I stopped the yoga and the tap-dancing lessons. I kept up my good eating habits. I continued going to my trainer, Kris, who was an ex-bouncer and club kid. He was a break-dancer and a karate master. He always knew if I'd skipped breakfast.

If I was super catty and mean to him, he understood it meant I was following the meal plan he'd given me and didn't take offense. He called me Sarcastro because of my sarcastic nature. He and I would work out and talk shit about people who were too dumb to realize how funny we were. No one was more proud of my weight loss than Kris. He helped me to realize how physically strong I was and could be. He taught me the importance of breakfast! (Seriously, I hate breakfast. I spent so many years waiting until I was alone to eat that I don't even get hungry until around two-ish. On some days, four-ish. My metabolism was as slow as molasses until I started eating breakfast. Now look at me! I'm still fat . . . and rich! Fuck you!) Kris found that I was a strong swimmer, so we would do workouts in pools sometimes, and I loved it. I started walking to the gym and back home afterward. It was a mile each way, so I was really on my grind.

One day Lee called me and asked how working out was going. I told him how great I felt and that I was now sixty pounds down from when he hired me. He was impressed. But then he said, "So, Gab . . . we're going to have to do reshoots for the film soon. How different do you look from Precious?" I sent him pictures. I looked different. Lee instructed me to stop working out until reshoots were over. The next week he called me, and carefully said, "Precious, I think if you concentrated and maybe ate some cake, it could really help us. You've lost too much weight." This was a sentence I'd never heard directed at me. I immediately started bragging about it instead of paying attention to the literal weight of what was being asked of me. I reversed everything that I'd been doing over the last nine months and tried to put weight back on. I didn't actually gain enough by the time I had to shoot again. In fact, it's pretty noticeable in the film. There's a fight scene where I look big, and then in the next scene I'm noticeably smaller and have darker skin (I had a tan from walking to the gym every day). In the next scene, I'm bigger and lighter again. Even without re-gaining all the weight, I did completely screw up all my prog-ress. I fell back into eating like an asshole. Skipping breakfast for chicken wings and french fries in the afternoon, and eating cake all the time because I "deserved it."

People have a lot of weird misconceptions about bigger peo-ple. I already knew that, but I knew it for sure when I started traveling to film festivals. I can't tell you how many times I had to hear, "I have to admit something. I thought that fat people were stupid, I thought they were lazy, and I thought they smelled bad. But meeting you, I realize that you're a nor-mal person like me. And you smell really good and you're so smart!" What the fuck, right? People not only thought it, but they thought it was appropriate to mention it to me. Inter-viewers saw fit to ask me if I ever thought about losing weight. As if 1) it hasn't been on my mind every waking moment of my entire life, and as if 2) it's any of their business.

Precious and *The Blind Side* were released the same year. Both were nominated for Oscars for best film and both fea-tured bigger people than we are used to seeing star in films. One was me, a woman (duh), and the other a man, Quin-ton Aaron. Truthfully, we were probably very near the same weight. He is tall and handsome, and part of me thought (thinks) we could be good friends. But back then I made the mistake of googling the comments about myself and comparing them to the comments section of Quinton's IMDb page. I was called a "Fat Fuck," "Fat Bitch," "Whale," "Gorilla," "Elephant." I was "ugly," "uglier," and, finally, "the ugliest." I was a "planet-sized bitch," "the BP oil spill," "dark as midnight," and don't even get me started on the "fat nigger" comments. Some people were "truly just concerned about" my weight. I was "a heart attack waiting to happen." People were predicting that I would "die any minute" and "won't make it to her 30th birthday." A lot of people were concerned that I was "promoting unhealthy eating habits." Funny, I could've sworn I was promoting a movie. Quinton was described as "ridiculously handsome" and a "big teddy bear with beautiful brown puppy dog eyes." I was pissed! I was so hurt that when I met him I was mean to him. I had no choice! Junior high school rules took over! He told me that he cried while watching *Precious,* and I replied, "Oh. Like a pussy?" He was really sweet and pleased to meet me so I immediately felt bad about saying something rude. So I only said like two more mean things. He remained sweet and humble. I'm not even sure he realized I was shading the shit out of him. He was really nice. And handsome. Damn those puppy dog eyes. Whenever I see him now, I try not to dwell over how differently we're received by the public. It's not his fault. Besides, that other shit is just business. The business of being different and being a woman at the same time. Don't even get me started on the many times I've been questioned about where I get my confidence.

I sometimes get so mad at myself. Mad at my body. I call it "my personal 9/11" when I am feeling really down. My body sometimes feels like a tragedy. But I'm trying very hard to change my mind about that. This is my body. It's going to be with me forever. For all the ways it's failed me, it's come through for me a million times more. I'll never be skinny and don't really want to be. I want to be smaller and I want to be healthier. My body will get me there. Every day I have to remind myself to be good to my body and allow it to be good to me. I'm also trying to stop my urge to make the joke first. I know my body is not funny. I choose me and my body over my fear of someone making a joke of it.

The urge to throw up is always there. The same way the depression is always there. But my struggles do *not* equal weakness. I'm pretty strong and will remain strong. I'm smart enough to get help when I start to lose myself to my emotions.

But there's no ending. Food is not a habit that I could ever kick. If I was addicted to heroin, I could go to rehab. Maybe wean off it with methadone or Jesus Christ. But it's food. I can't stop eating food. I need it to survive. I guess you can make the same argument for heroin, but still: I'll never be able to stop eating cold turkey (yum), which means that I'll never not struggle with my weight, and I'll never not grapple with the notion that I *could* just go throw up after I eat. Food's just going to keep on being delicious. As long as I have emotions, it'll be my first instinct to change them with banana pudding or macaroni and cheese. (And as long as there is Twitter, I *will* have emotions yo.) I'm struggling to find the healthy balance between food, feelings, and actual hunger while people on social-media sites continue to make fun of me. Meh. Fuck 'em. I'm prettier than they are anyway.

12

TWELVE SIXTY-SIX

Hello?

— Becky

WHEN I GRADUATED from my six months of dialectical behavioral therapy, I was twenty-one years old and completely unemployable. I started seeing a therapist once a week, but besides that, there was nothing else to fill my time. I'd been in about five different psych classes prior to and during my depression. So I was hella expert at therapy! (I use the term *expert* loosely!) I couldn't go back to City College because my grades had taken a nosedive during my depression. My GPA was so low that I wasn't allowed to register for any classes unless I had a meeting with the dean to explain what happened. Convincing the dean that I was worthy of a second chance was the only way I was going to be allowed to continue my education at my dream school (it had taken me a year and a half at Borough of Manhattan Community College to earn a place at City). I ended up telling him that I had become sick with a brain disease. I meant to say "depression" but it came out "brain disease." I immediately regretted it, because I felt as if I were misleading him into thinking I had a tumor or brain cancer. But I was more comfortable with him assuming either of those things than I was with saying, "*Um* . . . I don't know. I just got sad for a while." The dean seemed to know what I meant anyway. He asked if I was okay now. I told him that I was and that I was excited finally to get back to working on becoming a college graduate. He signed the paperwork I needed to re-enroll. Relieved, I left his office and went to register for class. When I got to the registrar's office, I was made aware of the fact that I had lost my financial aid. I couldn't use my mother's low income anymore to qualify, and the bill for my classes was . . . I don't remember. It was years ago. I just know it was more than what I had, which was nothing. The woman helping me could see the terror on my face. She took pity on me and advised me to wait until I was twenty-four to go back to school. She said that then I could use my own tax statement to apply for financial aid. At the age of twenty-four, I'd be considered an adult financially. I asked if I should consider a student loan, and she said, "No. I advise you to get a job and wait." For three years? Adulthood felt forever away. After all the work I'd done in therapy to grow as an adult, it felt like I was right back to being a nine-year-old kid again. Pissed off and ready to be grown.

I searched for a job for weeks. Months. But since I had very little work experience, no offers came my way. To be fair, I was completely unqualified for most jobs that didn't involve flipping burgers. All I had under my work-experience belt was an unsuccessful one-day stint selling knives during my freshman year of college. Not just any knives! Cutco knives! The World's Finest Cutlery (according to Cutco). You may know them as the knife set *not* sold in stores (for some reason) that features a pair of scissors sharp enough to cut a penny in half. My first sales call was to Crystal's mother, and I had a panic attack while trying to cut the penny and couldn't stop crying. I knew this wouldn't count as job experience at places like Forever 21, and it didn't, but I had also tutored an eight-year-old girl named Kaitey for about two years. She could barely read when I first started working with her, but her mom just tweeted me that Kaitey recently graduated in the top of her class from nursing school! Am I a wonderful person for teaching a child to read? Obviously! I'm basically Jesus. But does that make me employable? Apparently not.

I asked my therapist what she thought I should do. Therapists never really tell you what you should do. They ask you what *you* think you should do. If they know the correct answer, they hold it close to their vests as if they were in a poker match in a way that lets you know, "I'm here to listen, but you will be fucking up your life on your own, kiddo." My therapist told me that I was smart and that she knew I'd make the right decision for myself and to be patient and not think of myself as a loser. To be fair, I was twenty-one years old, lived at home in a crowded two-bedroom apartment, couldn't afford to go to school, and couldn't get a job. Plus, I had a six-month gap in my life spent learning to not solve my problems by sticking my fingers down my throat, an educational and workplace hiatus not easy to explain to prospective employers. Was she *sure*

I wasn't a loser? She said she was, and she suggested I get a job as a hostess or waitress. She asked if I had computer skills and suggested I try telemarketing. I knew that jobs hosting and waiting was a market cornered by actors and models, but telemarketing felt like something I could probably do. I was great over the phone. I had a pleasant speaking voice that didn't at all match what I look like in person. I thought a job over the phone would probably be ideal until I remembered my failure to sell anything to people without crying.

Listen, I could lie to you and say that I happened upon phone sex by accident while looking for telemarketing jobs, but who would that fool? We're friends now! You know me! As soon as my therapist suggested "telemarketing," I heard "phone sex." Must be my brain disease.

I liked reading the *Village Voice* for its articles about art shows, concerts, and stories about people living "alternative" lifestyles. (When can we stop calling gay people "alternative"? Now, please?) But the best part was the back page. The classifieds! There were all kinds of weird help-wanted and sex-toy ads back there, and I loved reading them. I knew that was where I'd find a listing for the only job I thought I could get. I'm not sure how the ad was worded. It may have said, "Phone actress." I know it said, "No experience necessary." Base pay and the potential to make fifteen dollars an hour. Yasss! I called the number provided. A woman answered and gave me an appointment to interview to be a "talker" for the following day.

Honestly, I thought I'd be walking into a dungeon with girls in ripped underwear chained to radiators who were moaning into receivers in phone booths. (If that's what I thought this job would be like, why was I showing up for the interview?

Desperation. Duh!) I was surprised when I stepped off the elevator to see a normal-looking office. There was a glass door separating the elevator from the actual office, and through it, I could see a young, handsome Puerto Rican man at the security desk wearing a T-shirt and jeans. He buzzed me in and asked who I was there to see. I assumed that the radiators and phone booths were at the back of the office. I was led into what seemed to be a conference room with bright-construction-paper-framed pictures of employees on the wall. Motivational messages and inspirational quotes on colorful banners were hung from the ceiling. This office seemed more like an elementary school classroom than what I thought a phone sex office would look like. More than likely, I borrowed clothes from my mom for the interview, something I thought would look professional, but everyone there was in a T-shirt and jeans. Even the young woman leading the interview, who introduced herself as Gina. A pretty, dark-skinned, and heavy-set woman, she looked busy, as if she had a lot of responsibilities. I thought the interview would be the normal one-on-one that I'd grown accustomed to before being thanked for my interest in the position only to never hear from the interviewer again, but this time I sat down with two other women much older than I was who were also being interviewed to be phone sex operators. I remember silently praying that I would have it figured out by the time I was either of their ages. I felt better about being there because I was still only twenty-one and had time to turn it around. I remember listening to their voices and thinking that neither of them sounded very sexy.

First, we talked numbers. I learned that this particular company had been in business for about fifteen years and was one of the more successful lines. The talkers made a base pay of seven dollars an hour, but if you were a good talker, you could potentially make up to fifteen dollars an hour in commissions. Commissions usually broke down to about ten cents a minute for every phone call. After ten minutes, though, commissions doubled to twenty cents a minute and tripled to thirty cents a minute after thirty minutes, and so on. There were other ways to boost commissions. If you were a good talker and a caller liked you enough to request you by name, you made two dollars before you even said hello.

Then we learned how to "talk." The interview turned into a forty-five-minute workshop about what to say and what not to say to a caller. Tips on how to answer a caller's questions included: the caller will tell you what he wants you to say and all you have to do is listen and then say it. For instance, if the caller says, "Are you wearing something sexy?" the answer is "Yes." He told you by asking the question that he wants you to say you're wearing something sexy. Gina informed us that phone sex isn't about getting the caller off. It's about stalling the caller so you can make money. You don't want to just pick up the phone and start moaning so the caller gets . . . done and then hangs up. A good talker makes the caller forget he's paying to talk to you. A good talker makes her answers as long as possible to keep the money rolling in. "Are you wearing something sexy?" "OMG! I am! It's new, too! I went on a shopping spree with my roomie yesterday! We're the same size in panties, but my boobs are bigger than hers, and I borrowed a bra from her and stretched it out so we went shopping for more bras, and I saw this super-cute lacy teddy. It's red with black bows on the bottom with these straps that hook to my panties and OH! So these panties make my butt look like a heart when I bend over! They're black satin with lace around the sides, and the seat of the panties is mesh, and you can see through it so . . . if I open up my legs! But I'm wearing a silk robe over my teddy because I just had a visitor. My weird neighbor knocked on my door to ask to borrow milk. Really? Milk? He's like obsessed with me. It's so weird. What are *you* wearing?" Okay, so I'm jumping ahead here, but see what I did there? If that guy's not already coming or whatever, he might want to know more about that roommate. He might want to know more about those panties and maybe even that weird neighbor. If the caller is freaky, he might want to know more about that milk.

Gina told us what we *shouldn't* say to a caller, too. That there were FCC rules and regulations that meant we couldn't discuss certain things on the phone. We couldn't mention anything of a sexual nature pertaining to anyone under the age of eighteen. We couldn't talk about drugs of any kind, prescription or illegal. No weapons of any kind, no blood or guts or gore. A lot of men would call and say, "My stepdaughter is eight," and the talker had to say, "Let's keep the party for people above the age of eighteen. I won't talk about anyone under that age of eighteen." (Talker tip: repeat yourself whenever possible to keep those minutes up.) Some men would then say, "My stepdaughter is eight . . . teen." Creep. But just so you know, there is more than likely no stepdaughter at all. No wife. Every call is about a fantasy. However gross and upsetting it may be, it's almost never real. If a caller wants you to stab him or he wants to stab you, you politely decline and make him aware of the rules. You can scratch and spank, but no wounds and no bleeding. Some callers want to be choked to death. You offer to choke them until they pass out, but they are to remain alive.

Another rule was that you, the talker, were not allowed to be any race other than good ol' American WHITE! The average caller is a white male. After oppressing the rest of the world all day, that white dude wants to go home, call a phone sex line, and talk to girls he's seen in porn or on TV. The average porn or TV actress is white. According to what I had already seen at this particular company, the average talker was a plus-size black woman. That's right, white dudes! You might think you're talking to Megan Fox, but you're actually talking to . . . well . . . ME! The majority of callers expect you to be white, but there are times when you get to be other races.

There are times when you get to act out any and every fantasy. Phone sex is like Netflix for the horny! And it's all got a label:

Barely legal: Talker is to be eighteen to nineteen years old. She's horny.

College girl: Talker is between eighteen and twenty-one years old. She's also horny.

Dom girl: Talker is a dominant mistress who orders the caller around and makes him do embarrassing things like wear girlie panties and laughs at the caller's tiny penis. Weird thing is, she's horny.

Submissive girl: Talker is willing to do everything her master, the caller, asks of her. You're not going to believe this, but she's horny.

Horny housewife: Talker is any age twenty-five and up, and also married. Also, super horny.

Mature: Talker is age forty and up. Coincidentally, she's hella horny.

Trans girl: Talker is a sexy lady with a huge penis. The bigger the better because the white male caller will want to suck it. That makes her so fucking horny.

Latina girl: YES! Guess who doesn't have to pretend to be white for once?! You're a sexy Latina from any country you choose! Maybe you're American born, maybe you moved to America from Argentina to pursue modeling because you're so pretty! Maybe you have an accent? Maybe you're in America because you're too horny for the men in your own country! Have fun with it! I almost always said I was Brazilian!

And last, but also least in popularity.

Ebony girl: GIRL! You made it! Are you horny? Yes? Then get yo black ass in here and tell this white male caller that he better not think about touching your hair! It hurt my heart to cut my words and suck my teeth in an effort to sound more "black" for the caller. I used to think maybe a caller who wanted an ebony girl was a shy businessman who worked at a firm for a black woman and had a crush on her but couldn't cross the professional line and ask her out. Maybe he thought she wouldn't be interested in dating a white boy. So he called chat lines to talk to black women to help boost his confidence so that one day he'd gain the nerve to actually ask her on a date. Fantasy works for everyone. Not just the callers.

But hold on! I didn't have the job yet! We were still at the interview/training workshop. Now it was time for the audition. We three talker candidates moved to a room set up with some desks obviously belonging to the women who worked in the training department, and across from those desks were what I would learn were "talking stations" — about four cubicles lined up one by one, each with a computer on a desk with headsets plugged into them. No receivers in telephone booths as I had suspected. The computer showed us how many talkers were on phone calls and how many talkers were available and waiting for callers. Gina was now joined by two more trainers, also plus-size black women, who would also be listening in and monitoring each of us on our calls. The older ladies and I were given names to use with the callers based on the sound of our voices. My twenty-one-year-old voice sounded about fifteen years old. Gina remarked, "Ooh, yeah, you sound really young and you got that high voice! They'll love you. Tell them your name is Becky." (Yes. Becky was my audition name.) The other women had deeper voices and therefore were given more mature names like Diane and Kathleen. We all sat at our stations and waited for our calls.

I was so pumped! I was nervous but mostly excited to put into practice all the tricks I had just learned in the training session. I was ready to listen and ready to be sexy! After about a minute, my phone rang and I picked up.

"Hello? This is Becky! Who's this?"

"My hand is on my cock and it's so hard!!!"

"Oh . . ."

My forty-five minutes of training left my brain in .045 seconds. I had no idea what to say! I was twenty-one years old! I wasn't a virgin, but I certainly wasn't some hot and horny temptress who knew exactly what to do with that hard cock. I didn't know what to do with it in person, and I didn't yet know what to do with it in a white-male fantasy. I mean, *damn!* Where was the romance? I didn't think I'd have to just get in there and start pretending to . . . wait. It flashed into my brain that Gina had given us very clear instructions that every call should start by getting the caller's name, location, and age. I was already behind on all of that. I overheard both the older ladies on their own calls and I panicked. I had to catch up. I started all over again.

"Hi! I'm Becky. What's your name?"

Click.

I lost him. He hung up on me. My very first caller wasn't having any of my "Hi! I'm Becky" bullshit. The trainers all looked at me and shrugged. Three more calls came through for Becky. Neither of them lasted more than a minute. I wasn't sexy and I couldn't even pretend to be. One of the older ladies who had been on a call for twelve minutes was told that she got the job. I knew that I would not be hearing that. Finally, Gina said to me, "Okay, you're done." I took the headset off so that I could hear that I wasn't getting the job, but just as it touched the desk, Becky got another call. I looked at Gina, and she said, "It's okay. Take it."

"Hello? This is Becky! Who's this?"

"Hi, Becky. This is Connie."

It was a woman. A woman! A female caller is actually really rare. Women don't pay for sex in any form with the frequency that men do. Women buy sex toys and watch porn, yes. But they don't usually invest in prostitutes or phone sex lines. I didn't know why Connie was calling, but I was glad she did. We ended up talking about Victoria's Secret bras for more than forty minutes. (Talker tip: Women are the easiest calls because once you start talking about sexy stuff with a lady caller it feels normal to go off on a tangent about what the best way to get a stain out of silk might be, because who has time to run to the cleaners for one little spaghetti stain? Like do you even know how often I get stuck at work because my stupid boss makes me recount all the twenty-dollar bills in the petty-cash drawer over and over again at the end of the day? I mean HELLO! Just because he has OCD doesn't mean I have to miss spin class, right? See that? Tangent!) I forget how the call ended. I think Connie just ran out of time or something. I don't think she got off. I'm going to be honest with you; I have no idea how to get a woman off. I know I have lady parts so theoretically I should know, but I don't. I know what gets me off, but I can't be sure that delicious pizza and being left alone to play *The Sims* on my laptop will do it for other women.

When the call was over, both the older ladies had gone. I was offered the job! I felt I had really accomplished something! It had yet to dawn on me that the accomplishment involved men breathing heavily into my ear. The trainers explained to me that every girl who becomes a talker is assigned a number. The numbers are in chronological order, and if I left the company for any reason and then came back, my number would remain. My number was 1266 because I was the company's 1,266th employee. Theoretically speaking, my number is still 1266. If a caller wanted to request me, he would be able to do it by number and/or by name because there were never two girls with the same name working for the company at the same time even though talker names were recycled. Gina asked me what I wanted my name to be. I chose Melody, figuring I had the melodic high-pitched voice to pull it off. I was Melody, girl 1266.

One of the trainers walked me over to human resources. YES! There was a human resources department. This was a real place of business! Isn't that weird? I met with another plus-size black woman; this office was beginning to look like my family reunion. She gave me a packet of paperwork to fill out and explained to me that they couldn't offer me a medical plan. This meant nothing to me as I was still, remember, twenty-one years old. She explained the rules of the company and made me aware that I was on probation for the first three months of my employment there. She informed me that working at the company would be a fun experience as there were random tea parties and holiday celebrations all the time. Every girl's birthday was celebrated, and there were lots of games talkers played to boost morale. Each talker had the ability to gain "stars" for calls longer than ten minutes. Stars could be saved up and then turned in for Best Buy and Target gift cards and other prizes. There were talkers who saved stars to buy Christmas presents and furnish their homes. The HR woman took me on a tour of the office. I met the receptionist and the supervisors. I met the operators. Operators are not talkers. They take the callers' credit card information and then put them through to the talker requested. (Talker tip: Make friends with the operators. If a caller requests a girl who isn't currently at work, an operator can suggest that the caller try a new girl. You! They'll send you a note detailing what the guy is into, and when you get the request . . . that's right! You make two dollars before you even say hello! But operators only do this for their friends. Remember this.) I was showed the nap room. This was a twenty-four-hour, seven-days-a-week company. We were open on New Year's and Christmas and every major holiday in between — those days paid time and a half, which meant you could make $22.50 an hour. You could choose your own hours, working from 9 a.m. to 5 p.m. for a more traditional workday or 8 a.m. to 8 p.m. if you preferred. Even better, 8 p.m. to 8 a.m., when the base pay shot up to nine dollars an hour. For those who liked to work overnight, falling asleep was a real hazard, so you could reserve some time in the nap room and spend your hour-long break in there taking a snooze before you got back on the phones. This was going to be an amazing place to work. I asked how I could apply for a position other than talker. I was informed that every woman at the company started out as a talker and that while it takes years to move up in the company it could, in fact, happen if I worked hard enough. But when the HR woman introduced me to Girl 150 who was still just a talker, I got how long it could take to move up in the company. What hope did Girl 1266 have? I was sent home to develop a life and character for Melody as if I'd be with her a long time.

I started work the next day. I was given a headset with my number etched into the side of it. Branded. In the supervisors' office, where I punched in, there were always two supervisors on duty along with a receptionist. Always a man and a woman. I walked down the hall to my locker to put my purse away (actually, I still wore backpacks back then as if I were forever on my way to third-period science class). The talker floor was a huge dark room filled with cubicles. One side of the room had windows but that didn't matter as the shades were always drawn to ensure twenty-four-hour darkness on the floor. There were usually about thirty to forty talkers working at a time. They sat in cubicles lined up one by one in about six rows with a computer sitting on every other desk. A talker never sat directly next to another girl because the caller wasn't supposed to overhear the next talker. For the first week of work, I was to sit in the talker representative section. This is where the expert talkers sat and trained new talkers and helped them adjust to sucking a dick over the phone. These women I cannot remember by name, but their numbers are still as clear as day to me. Numbers 2, 5, 10, and 20 all helped me on my first week of talking. These women had been with the company since the beginning. They made the most money on the phones because the majority of their calls were requests from the same customers they'd been talking to since the '90s. Number 2 was a Trinidadian woman with a slight accent on the phone but a thick "What the fuck did she just say?" accent in real life. She was the OG of the talker floor. If you were talking too loudly, she'd come directly to you and tell you to "quiet ya mouff!" Number 10 was much sweeter and my favorite, frankly. She was a black British woman. I would listen to her coo her accent into the ears of men who had been calling her for a decade. Every call was like a reunion for her. The majority of women on the talking floor were mothers. Some were college students who needed flexible hours. Most had more than this one job. Some were also strippers or dominatrices. Some were just there to make extra Christmas money for their grandchildren. Most, no matter their background, had been there for way too long, and none of them had moved up in the company. From the beginning, I was scared that I'd be there too long myself, picking up calls in the year 2020 from people I'd been talking to since 2005.

The company was founded by a husband and wife, a white couple who were almost never in the office. They were usually on their way to a cruise or just coming back from a cruise. The company's staff was 95 percent women. Most of these women were black. Any woman who held a job title above talker was a smart, problem-solving woman with a huge list of responsibilities. There were a few men who worked at the company, all as supervisors or doing clerical work or as security. Each one of them was connected to a woman or women who worked there. A husband, a son, a boyfriend of a talker. Men were only hired after a woman who worked at the company vouched for them. When the phones were really busy, no matter what was going on or what department they were in, all of these smart black women had to get on the phones and pretend to be stupid young white girls for the pleasure of white men. The irony wasn't lost on me. Or anyone else there, for that matter. That's why we were all constantly being distracted by games to collect stars to turn into gift cards to buy stuff with. Everything was about how much money we could make so that we didn't have to take a look at what we were really doing. It worked for me and it worked *on* me. But I told myself I wasn't degrading myself for some faceless caller. He was the one paying to get all sticky and gross while listening to me recite *Cosmo*'s latest list of ways to give the perfect blow job. I was safely in a cubicle in a nice office building flipping through magazines and making a decent amount of money while pretending to be a gorgeous white girl named Melody with daddy issues. Sure, there were a lot of calls that were gross and degrading in a way that I couldn't shake off. But what was I supposed to do? Quit? It had taken me so long to find this job in the first place. Quitting would just take me back to square one. I couldn't afford that. In order to not walk away from the phones feeling tired and dirty, I had to allow myself to be convinced that I had the upper hand.

My therapist had an opinion about my new job. She didn't think it was a good idea. She thought it was psychologically damaging and hurtful to all the work I'd done to get over my depression. I knew that she was right on one level, but I was actually really happy at that job. I was good at it, which gave me a sense of accomplishment, and I was able to afford to help my mom out with the rent, which made me feel productive. I was able to go out with my friends and not worry about how I was going to pay for dinner. I could afford to have fun. I couldn't let what I said on the phones be real to me. Most of what I said and heard was hilarious, and it made me laugh. A lot. I was making fun of those men as soon as I hung up. If I was on a domination call, I'd make fun of them while still on the call. Also, I don't want you to think that every caller was some terrible creepy man rubbing himself and wanting me to call him Daddy. When I first started taking calls, I worked Saturday nights from 8 p.m. to 8 a.m. for the bump in pay, and the majority of calls that came in were from soldiers stationed in Afghanistan. Those soldiers were very polite and lonely. Not one of them wanted me to pretend to give them a blow job. They didn't call for sex at all. They called because they wanted to talk to someone who wasn't their family. For one, their loved ones were usually asleep at that time of night. But also they didn't want to talk to people who missed them. Who were worried about them and wanted them to come home. One soldier explained to me that it was emotionally taxing to talk to someone you missed, who missed you, too. That wanting to be there for that loved one and hearing about all the things you were missing out on could make a person feel worse than they felt before they started talking. We talkers were paid to pick up the phone and be nice. That's it. The average soldier would stay on a call for more than an hour. Sometimes two hours, until his prepaid card was out of minutes. The talker and the caller can hear when the system is going to cut the call off. At the end of the call, a soldier would always say, "Ma'am, it's been real nice talking to you, so thank you for being kind. And remember when you go to bed tonight that we're out here fighting for your freedom and fighting to make sure you're safe."

As I mentioned, the average caller was not a creepy old man with his hands on his balls. He was someone who just wanted to talk to a girl he imagined was pretty who wouldn't reject him . . . and Charlie Sheen. Yes, a lot of calls were from creepy men who called me a bitch and a slut as I pretended to love it. It absolutely could be degrading work no matter how many "nice guys" called in.

My therapist was having none of it. She really thought I should reconsider this job. I asked her again what she thought I should do. She sighed very deeply, and said to me, "Gabby. I think that you are smart. You're very smart and you know what this line of work can do to you. I believe you can figure out a way to stop it and still get what you want." I said okay without really knowing what I was saying okay to.

About a month and a half after I started working at phone sex, I turned twenty-two. I didn't work on my birthday, but a few days after, a supervisor called me into the conference room at around two in the morning. I followed her in, and the trainers, supervisors, and receptionist presented me with balloons, a card, and a box of chocolates for my birthday. The card was signed by multiple talkers, most of whom I didn't even know. I was surprised, because I'd mostly kept to myself and hadn't made friends yet. I thanked them all and went back to the phones. During my lunch break at around 4 a.m., I went into the break room to read my book. *Terrifying Tales* by Edgar Allan Poe. The supervisor who'd called me in for the surprise birthday moment saw me reading and asked if I read a lot. Then she asked what I did for my birthday. I told her, and she asked me a few more questions about myself. After I answered them, she remarked that I was smart and went back to her desk. I remember thinking that if I was as smart as she and my therapist said I was, I would've been able to find a job where I didn't have to hear the word *cock* a hundred times a day. The next day the same supervisor called me into the conference room again. I expected more balloons, but the room was empty. She sat me down and informed me that one of the receptionists was leaving the company and said that if I wanted the position it was mine. I'd been working for less than two months and already I was being given a promotion! Receptionists made twelve dollars an hour. Technically speaking, I had the potential to make more money as a talker, but as a receptionist I didn't have to pretend to blow anyone, so it was a better job. I was off the talker floor. (Maybe I am smart?) My receptionist training began that same day. The rumors that I was a lesbian who'd slept my way to the promotion also started the next day.

Things can sometimes work out if you're smart, but my greatest virtue is patience. I had a demeaning job that required me to pretend I was sucking a dick over the phone every day. Even after my promotion to receptionist, if the phones were busy, I had to leave my desk and go back to the talker floor and pretend to be an empty-headed girl for some creep to jerk off to. It wasn't ideal, but I was eventually promoted again and again and again until I began training to be the person who interviewed hopeful applicants. I was becoming Gina. I was with the company for three years. I was patient enough to turn the degradation into something positive. I took what I learned on the phones about secrets, shame, and pleasure, and applied it to the real world around me. I learned how to talk to people. I learned how to flirt with everyone and everything. I learned to lead with my personality. I learned to deal with rumors. (If the girls on the talker floor thought I got a promotion by being a lesbian, I let them. All the lesbians I know are dope and get shit done. I've certainly been called worse!) I learned to boldly ask for what I wanted. I learned that your average businessman works hard and carries plenty of shame as well as self-entitlement. (Also, he might be wearing panties under his suit and that's *his* business.) I'm not afraid to say anything to anyone. I'm not afraid to *be* anyone. I've already experienced the worst of people, and I've learned that we're all still human. My patience taught me to survive as 1266, and my intelligence helped me say yes to acting when the opportunity was presented to me.

I've had acting roles that I felt demeaned me as much if not more than the phone sex calls. I took those roles because it was my job to take them and because the relationships and experience I've gained will eventually allow me to create and play my own characters. I want to tell my own stories, and someday soon I will.

13

IS THIS A DATE?

"If you're looking at me, I'm your type!"
— Dizzy Moore (BFF)

FULL DISCLOSURE, I DON'T KNOW dick about dating. I started doing it pretty late in life. Nineteen. I was basically a grandmother. I know that you're probably thinking, *Oh, right! You didn't date before you were nineteen because of the . . . "fat thing,"* huh? First of all, there's no need to whisper. Yes, I was a fat child and then a fat teenager, but boys liked me. Probably not as many as liked the thin girls, but I was really funny, and I was cool. I knew every rap song on the radio and every lyric DMX ever wrote (this was very sexy and solidified me as a catch . . . in my own mind). I could sing; I always had my own money, so I never begged for some boy to buy me a Snickers or anything; and I was generous and fun to be

around. I'm not saying I was beating boys off with a stick, but
I had admirers.

In the seventh grade, a boy sent me a note one Friday asking
me out. (It's important to know that in junior high a guy "asking you out" means asking you to be his girlfriend. There is no
actual going *out* required.) After school, I had a friend send a
note back to him saying yes. We didn't have each other's phone
numbers and didn't know where the other lived so we didn't
speak over the weekend. On Monday morning, I sent my new
boyfriend a note that said, "It's dead." We never spoke again.

When I was in the eighth grade, a ninth grader asked me to
be his date to the prom. This was a big deal because it meant
that I'd be the only one of my friends who'd get to go to prom
a year early. That's some Kelly Kapowski shit right there. I said,
"Yeah! Cool." About a week later, my date asked me if I'd
bought my dress yet and what color it was so that he could get
me a corsage that matched. At this point I realized I was afraid
of prom. PROM! Do you even know what goes on there? You
have to put on a dress and makeup. MAKEUP! And you have
to dance. Not just by yourself but with the dude who brought
you there. IN FRONT OF EVERYONE! Also, since you'd be
there with that dude, he probably liked you, and you probably
liked him, so everyone would know you had FEELINGS for
that guy! ICK! And then at the end of the night you'd probably have to let him kiss you! Your ample bosom would heave
up and down in anticipation; it would be like all of a sudden
you're in a romance novel. And then you'd have to meet his
family, and he'd have to meet yours, and then you'd settle for
him and get married, and then you'd be just as unhappy as
your mom when she was married.

This was all happening too fast. BAIL. ABORT MISSION. I looked down at my feet, and said, "I don't really have time to find a dress. Go with someone else." Then I walked away bravely. Okay. Maybe not bravely. I was scared. Not of prom, but of boys. I was scared of relationships in general. I'm not sure what boys and relationships represented for me back then, but I didn't want any part of it. Meanwhile, my junior high crew of black girls my age with first names ending with the letter *a* were all boning boys. My best friend was only technically a virgin, and my other friends already had a designated room in the school's basement where they'd go get it on. But for me, even the idea of dancing with a boy was enough to make me shut down.

My fear of boys, however, did nothing to stop me from being completely boy crazy. I was always desperate to grab the attention of some boy, usually the kid with the worst grades and the most behavioral problems. Any boy who'd curse out the teacher, throw a chair, get suspended, and then still show up to school at three o'clock smoking a cigarette to meet up with his boys—be still my slow-beating heart. But even when one of those kinds of boys asked me out or told me to meet him in the basement, I'd pretend I hadn't heard and I'd never show up. I only talked a pretty good game. I was flirty, I made goo-goo eyes and giggled, but I couldn't handle anything more.

I certainly wasn't going to let anyone know I thought I was good enough to be someone's girlfriend. Why? So that everyone could tell me that I wasn't? If I admitted to myself that I liked some dude, I'd immediately figure he was out of my league; and even though I was fun and cute and essentially a good person, in my mind the guy would be way cuter. After all, if I said, "Yes, I'll go out with you" to some guy, all he'd have to say was "EWW! Hell, no! I was joking." Everyone would laugh, and furthermore, they'd know that I liked that boy. That I could have those kinds of feelings. Love feelings.

"Love feelings"? What *am* I? A robot from a future where love has been outlawed? What the hell is wrong with me? Why can't I communicate intelligently about love? I'm a human being. I'm comfortable talking about pain. I'm comfortable talking about self-love. But the concept of romantic love feels weird and kind of foreign in my brain. I guess I'm figuring out that I wasn't just afraid of relationships as a child but that I'm still afraid of them as an adult.

I'm still pretty boy crazy. My mom tells me to call them "men," but that seems too grown-up a word, and frankly, I'm not there yet. But to clarify, when I say "boys," I definitely mean age twenty-five or older. The boys I like now are less likely to throw a chair. They're producers, writers, directors, and sound engineers. They're artists. They have grown-up jobs and lives. They're kind of dorky and know a lot about specific subjects like film, the Civil War, Renaissance art, Africa, or how batteries work. See? I've grown up some! The boys I like now are my friends. We hang out and go to dinner or get drinks. We'll be at dinner, and I'll look at my friend and realize that this guy's a legit catch. He's handsome, nice, smart, polite, funny . . . I KNOW THE PERFECT GIRL TO SET HIM UP WITH. And then that's what I'll do. I'll set my friend up with a girlfriend of mine who I think can appreciate a guy like him. I'll give the perfect guy away. I swear I'm not even conscious of what I'm doing when I'm doing it. It's like I think to myself, *This guy's a keeper but not for you. Still, you shouldn't let him go to waste!* I guess I still think the guy is out of my league.

Honestly, let's talk leagues for a second. I swear, nothing has pushed my life off track like becoming an actress. Before that, I had my league perfectly figured out. I was going to marry a cabdriver, because my league included cabbies, sanitation workers, security guards, and maybe grocery-store managers. Now that I'm a Hollywood actress, my league is all messed up! I don't have to date only cabbies anymore, but I'm pretty sure I can't date the Liam Hemsworths and Michael B. Jordans, either. Maybe I can date a high school teacher or something? I don't know.

On one of my ask-Mom-personal-questions days, I called her and grilled her about the day she became Mrs. Sidibe.

"Is this gonna get me arrested?" she asked.

"I think there are probably statutes of limitation on immigration fraud from thirty-seven years ago. I think you're good. You're in the clear."

"Check before you publish this! I don't want to go to prison."

"Mom, y'all stayed married for like ten years, and you have two adult children now. I don't think it's fraud anymore."

"CHECK!"

"Okay, I'll check," I lied. She crazy. "Do you remember what you were wearing?"

"Nope." We both laughed.

"Did you have rings?"

"Nope."

"What'd you do after you got married?"

"He went back to his apartment and I went back to mine."

That's it. That's the tradition I have to follow. No flowers, no toasts. No party even. Mom didn't tell her parents about the marriage until nearly a year later when she was about to go to Africa with Dad. She introduced him to her parents so they could see he was a nice man.

Mom has told me before that she grew to care for my dad. But now I wanted it straight.

"Had you fallen in love with Dad?"

"No."

Long pause. Not because I was surprised, but because I could relate. I don't think I've ever been in love.

"Did you dream of what your wedding would be like as a kid?" I asked.

"No. Not really. My mother told me I'd never get married cuz I was fat. I was a little big girl, and you know, men didn't really like that then." (As if they love that shit today.) "So I didn't want to get married because I was told I'd never get married anyway. So I said, 'That's okay.' I had a voice. I was fine. I didn't dream about a wedding and a big gown . . . walking down the aisle."

There. There's my family tradition. Maybe if she had known that love and marriage weren't any less an option for her than anyone else, my mom could've taught that to me. But she didn't, because she wasn't taught that, and now neither of us know it. In a slight variation of what her mother told her —that no man would marry her until she lost weight—Mom told me that I would have to settle for a man I didn't love if I didn't lose weight. But I've already been through a marriage of settlement. Hers. I'd rather not do it again.

When I was twenty-four years old, I came close. Toward the end of that summer, I met a cabdriver while leaving work one night down at the phone-hoe factory. He drove me home, and then he didn't charge me but instead asked for my phone number. A free ride? Swoon. I suppose I gave it to him. He wasn't remarkably handsome, he had an accent I couldn't place, and if I'm remembering correctly, his name was Malik. He shared that name with both my father and one of my brothers, so I knew he was Muslim. He was a Yellow Cab driver just like Dad. Was he my type? I don't fucking know! But he texted to ask me out and I was bored, so I said yes. He said he'd pick me up. I hadn't gotten a good look at him when he drove me home so I wouldn't have been able to pick him out in a lineup of two people, and what's worse, he was in a cab. All the cars on my street were cabs! After much confusion, I figured out which driver of which cab was my date, and we went to some diner on the Upper West Side of Manhattan that I found to be grown-up and fancy. I was young and unfancy then. We talked over dinner and got to know each other. He was from Egypt. He was absolutely Muslim. He tried his best to be a good man. He wanted to get married. Just like the psychic said. I rolled my eyes through the part about getting married. While this guy was nice, he wasn't particularly interesting, and if I'd gone to the bathroom and come back to a completely different man sitting at our table, I wouldn't have noticed. I assumed that even though he'd brought up marriage he didn't mean me. How could he? We'd just met. Surely he was speaking generally, not specifically.

At the end of the night, he drove me home, and while we were still in his cab, he turned to me, and said, "I want to marry you." Swoon? I wasn't surprised or even caught off guard. I was annoyed. "You need a green card?" I asked. He seemed surprised. Idiot. Do you even *know* how smart I am and how big a cliché you are? "Yes," he admitted, as if no one else would have cracked the code of an immigrant asking a woman to marry him on the first date. "How did you know?" he asked, as if I were a psychic. "That's how my parents got married," I answered. "No, thank you. I gotta go." Then I got out of the cab and went to bed. The next day he texted me saying that he hadn't meant to offend me and that he really did like me. While I wasn't offended, I told him to cut the bullshit and said I wasn't interested in marriage fraud. But then he kept texting me. All day long. Then he asked if I wanted a ride home . . . the things I've done for a ride home. So we're in his cab again, and he starts to plead his case. He at first was coming at me in a romantic way as if I would believe that we were in love and that we should get married as soon as possible. When he saw that I wasn't falling for it, he decided to approach me as if we were going into business together. He explained that we wouldn't have to be married for that long. Two or four years. That I could move in with him in Queens and that he could pay me. Pay me? Swoon! That's when I really started to consider it. I took a few days to weigh my options. I even made a pros and cons list. I still lived with Mom and Ahmed in a two-bedroom apartment. Even with my job as a phone sex monitor, I wasn't making enough money to live on my own yet. I didn't know how or if I could ever move out. It felt like I was doomed to live at home forever and that poor Mom was also doomed to sleep in the living room forever because of it. I just had to leave. Maybe immigration fraud and a green-card marriage was my ticket. I thought maybe I'd move to Queens and have the cabdriver pay my way through school. By the time I was finished with school and placed firmly in whatever career I'd end up with, I'd be done with marriage. The idea of marriage was scary, but a sham marriage was just a sham! It wasn't forever. The only hiccup would be if I fell for the guy while we were married. Then I'd end up pregnant. But then I'd have a baby and that wouldn't be so bad because that's what was expected of me. I *was* a woman after all. Maybe this was just what my life would be. Unhappily married to an African cabdriver named Malik so that he could stay in this country. It was exactly what Mom had done. But Mom had gotten something out of it. She had a life. And she had proved her mother wrong! I was no better than Mom. Who was I to think that starting my life this way wouldn't be enough?

But . . . I couldn't let that bitch be right. Not this time. Mom is always right. She's right about many things, so it has been my lifelong crusade to make her wrong about *me*. I was forever swimming upstream. Throughout my life, she had been right about more things than I cared to remember, but she would lose this round. I refused to settle. Not just because she told me that I would have to and I wanted to prove her wrong, but also because this marriage would be EXACTLY what she'd done with Dad. *Exactly.* I was about to marry Dad! Something I had vowed to never do.

Problem is, I still wanted the things on the pro list. Not all of it. Not the things other people wanted for me like marriage and children, but the things I wanted, like an education and to move out of Mom's apartment so she could move into my bedroom. Independence. That's what I wanted. I wasn't sure how I would get it without marrying Malik. I didn't know how other people got it so I googled "How to go back to college." That's how I found Mercy College. I kept opening up page after page until I figured out how to apply for financial aid on my own now that I was old enough to do so. I enrolled myself for the upcoming semester. I was on my way back to school on my own three years after losing my aid at City College. I wouldn't need Malik to pay my way. I wouldn't need anyone. I called him and let him know that I was going to begin classes soon and that, along with my work schedule, I wouldn't have time to see him anymore. Also that I wouldn't be marrying him but that I wished him luck anyway. He was annoyed. He accused me of wasting his time, but his whole situation had nothing to do with me. Two weeks later I was back at school and two weeks after that I was a movie star, so none of it mattered anyway. I had turned down a marriage proposal about a month before I got my first film role. Change was in the air like a cloud and it was finally raining on me.

The idea of marriage remains very scary to me. A real marriage. One where you love each other. Where you have dreams of a future together with a home and children. Couple friends and game nights. Family vacations and studio portraits on the wall. One man for the rest of my life. That shit is scary. It's scary because I don't know what that looks like from the inside. My parents were only able to show me some of those things, but because they weren't in love with each other, was what they did show me even real? I want to love a man who loves me, but I don't really want to get any more involved than just that. I don't want to meet his family or have him meet mine. I just can't imagine melding my entire life with someone else's for eternity. Can't I just fall for a friendless orphan? Getting married is so fucking normal, and in the right case, a healthy way to grow. Normal? All of my instincts tell me to run the opposite direction.

Is it a surprise then that I have a knack for dating guys who clearly aren't interested in me? Guys I annoy. Who think I'm stupid and boring. Who think I'm mean and ugly. Who think they can do better than me but for some reason they aren't. Guys I think would love me if I could somehow prove my worth to them, but who, other than that, I'm not particularly interested in, either. This way we're *both* unhappy. It's called being an adult! Actually, it's called being stupid. Wasting my own time. I once had a three-year relationship with a guy who was mean to me all the time. He'd sit next to me, and I could feel his contempt wafting off him. Even his sighs sounded like he hated me.

Meanwhile, I couldn't wait for him to get the hell out of my apartment. He was young, stupid, and thought he was more attractive than he actually was. He lied about everything, and he was really a bad person. But there we were, both in this relationship, pretending to like each other. During this time, I was really close with another guy. We were mostly just friends. I'd ask him for advice all the time, basically doing that very girlie thing of asking a straight guy friend what to do about my relationship even though I knew the answers already. My friend knew that my boyfriend was an asshole, so he asked very seriously, "Do you think you deserve your life?"

I didn't understand, so he clarified his question.

"Okay, well, you know how you have a dream job starring

in movies and TV shows, and people think you're funny, and when we go to restaurants, the chefs always send over extra food because you're kind of a celebrity, and you get to travel the world first-class for free? Do you think that you deserve that?"

I considered the question very seriously, and after a moment, I answered, "No. Not really."

He smiled and took my hand in his, and said, "You keep your horrible boyfriend around because you feel like shit, and he's the only one around who agrees with you. He validates the part of you that thinks you deserve bad things instead of good things. When you start believing that you deserve good things, you'll dump him because he won't fit anymore. But for now, he treats you like shit because that's what you want."

It was like a punch in the face. A hard punch with a fist made of the truth. I did feel like shit a lot of the time. I felt unworthy of all the good things in my life, so keeping around a boyfriend who agreed with that felt . . . comforting. Really, he was a placeholder for a real boyfriend. If in his place there was a guy I was really attracted to and liked and respected, then I'd be forced to grow up and deal with all of the very real feelings and life choices that went along with loving someone in a romantic way. At the time, though, I wasn't ready to be a grown-up in that way.

Dating seems to conclude with something being wrong with me. I'm not sure the mental gymnastics are worth it. I mean, I guess sometimes you get a free dinner out of it, but I can buy my own dinners . . . I just don't want to. In fact, I'm not done with dating just because I'm tired of it. It's not even really my decision to stop. I'm being forced into retirement. I'm moving from New York City to LA, and dating in LA for a girl like me isn't just hard. It's impossible. This forced retirement is fine by me. I'm basically Danny Glover in *Lethal Weapon*. I'm too old for this shit.

Here's the thing about LA. I don't really want to move there. I figured I'd live my entire life in New York City and then die there. (Morbid, I know, but, spoiler alert, I'm going to die one day. You, too. You first, though.) But in my thirties, it's time for me to live comfortably with more space. Listen! I saw *Hamilton*, too, okay?! I love the shit out of New York City! But I'm tired of hearing my upstairs neighbors have sex. It feels like a super-inconvenient threesome. LA will be fine. I could use the room. In New York City everyone is stacked on top of one another like sardines. More room will be nice and will make saying good-bye to dating worth it. I think. LA is filled with trees, sunlight, houses with pools in the backyards, and gorgeous people working on their respective careers by looking to date other gorgeous people who can boost their careers. LA can be pretty superficial. I know I'm generalizing, but it seems that when the LA dudes I meet are showing interest in a girl like me it's usually for one reason.

When I say "a girl like me," I bet you think I'm just talking about being fat. How dare you fat-shame me!? You think I'm talking about being black? Racist! What makes you think I'm not talking about being smart? What? You don't think a fat black girl can be smart or something? Fat-shaming racists like you make me sick! Just kidding. I'm sure you're not a racist. I mean, you might be, but I can't know that for sure. Did you vote for Trump? Let's move on. When I say "a girl like me" I mean all of it, I guess. I am currently fat or plus-size. (I don't have a problem with the word *fat* because I'm dead inside now, but I know a lot of plus-size people do.) I am and forever will be black. (Thank GAWD! No shade.) I'm also smart. Look at me writing this whole book by myself! Wheeeee! I've found all three of those facts about me to be both a turn-on and a turnoff at some point or another. With other factors, like feeling the need to make a joke out of nearly everything, being always on time, looking younger than I actually am while seeming older than I actually am, being lazy, working really hard anyway, having my own money, knowing almost every song ever, and liking to sing the nonexistent harmonies of rap songs, the list of idiosyncrasies that make up my personality is vast and polarizing. Good, bad, and ugly, they're all me, and at some point, I've been asked out because of one or the other or dumped because of one or the other. But I guess we all have been. That's how being a human being on a planet of other human beings works, right?

But of all of my traits, negative or positive, nothing has ever been more polarizing than fame. I'm sure I've mentioned this before, but fame is super weird. It comes with a ton of perks like free appetizers and desserts, but because everyone thinks this is so fun and glamorous, you're not allowed to complain. But seriously, sometimes the only thing keeping me from eating a chocolate cake is the fact that it's not literally sitting in front of me. When I'm at a restaurant and decline to look at the dessert menu but then the manager sends over a huge slice of chocolate cake, it's like FUCK! Whose side are you on, manager dude? I came here for the salads! Stop ruining my life! Plus, it would be rude if I sent the cake back or didn't eat it, and my momma did *not* sing in the subway and raise me right to have me send a free piece of cake back! But see? I look like an asshole for complaining about free chocolate cake! There's no winning here. Fame is a double-edged sword, and there are so many kinds of chocolate cake to devour or avoid.

Much like chocolate cake, people started to show up in front of me just because of what I do for a living. That's usually fine. I'm in the business of entertainment, I meet other entertainers while I'm at work, and we often click because there's a common thread of understanding between us. That's cool. I have plenty of friends I wouldn't have met if I wasn't an actress, and I'm grateful to have them all. What sucks are the droves of attractive dudes who just kind of show up in one way or another in front of me and flirt with me and spend time with me only to hand me a script or ask me to post a picture of them on my social-media accounts in order to boost their followers. Can I complain about that? Please?

When I was boy crazy as a teenager, I guess I thought, *When we're adults, it won't be like this. We'll be too busy working and, plus, we'll be married by then!* (Yes, in my inner thoughts, I refer to myself as "we" and I, excuse me, *we* don't think that's weird.) Problem is, I'm busy and not married yet but, shit, I still have time to check out a package or two. Maybe age and business have nothing to do with my boy craziness. Maybe it's just another birth defect like my sarcasm and sassiness. Either way, if a cute dude starts flirting with me, I'm suspicious but also intrigued. This problem has worsened since I've become an actor, and as long as I have eyes and lady parts, it'll probably be a problem forever. I've told you how soon I put dudes into the friend zone, or rather I put myself in the friend zone and eliminate myself from the possibility of anything more. I'm working on it! In the meantime, the guys I *do* pay attention to are the ones overtly flirting with me and asking me out in a romantic way. Even I find those signs hard to ignore.

So I'll let them take me to dinner or drinks or whatever, and I get to play my least favorite game ever: the "Is This a Date?" game! Fun for no one! Here's how it goes. Flirty dude will text me some flirty/friendly shit a few times, and then say, "We should link up." Now the word *link* is some tricky Clinton administration number-one shit. It's language that makes it hard to tell what's actually happening. You can *link up* with your mom to celebrate her birthday, but you can also *link up* with the dweeb you cheat off of in science class to let him cop a feel under the bleachers. What exactly does *link up* even mean? Nobody knows! And you can't know until after the linkup! I once asked my straight friend who was helping me to text a dude I liked if I could change the language from "linkup" to something more clear like "hang out," and he looked at me like I was a murderer. When I asked if I could just be honest and say, "Come over and eat me out," he refused to help me anymore.

So then flirty dude is all like, "Meet me at this place for dinner." Dinner? Does he mean dinner or does he mean *dinner?* See?! So much confusing wordplay! Also, he said, "Meet me." If this was a date, he would've picked me up, right? This is where the real nonfun begins because you have to start adding and subtracting points. "Meet me" will cost this date five points. If he says, "What's your address, I'll pick you up," you can give the date ten points until you remember that your gay best friend and your straight platonic male friend also pick you up, so you dive deep into your own psyche and deduct ten points for being crazy before you even get in the car.

Once you're officially at the *linkup* (once you've *lunked?*), you can start to assess the situation at hand. Did he bring you anything? Flowers or something? A Snickers bar or a key chain from some other city he was just visiting? I ask because this has happened to me. A guy who truly did not want to bone me planned a *linkup* with me and brought me flowers and a cross from Canada, and it was confusing as fuck! You want to think, *Gifts! This is definitely a date! One hundred points!* But I assure you, flirty dude is definitely up to something sinister. Flowers? The fuck?! Deduct five hundred points.

When you're both looking over the menu and trying to decide what you want and if he orders the same exact item as you, flip the table and run out of there as fast as possible to escape that psychopath. Even if this *is* a date, you don't need that bullshit in your life. What kind of person sits down at a restaurant with another person and orders the same exact thing? This is a *restaurant,* homie! There are so many options! If I'm ordering something you want, it's your duty as an AMERICAN to get the second-most-desired item so that *we* can have both! Are you even serious right now? You think Jay Z and Beyoncé go to restaurants and order the same meal?! Deduct one thousand points! If he has some human decency and orders a different meal for both of you to enjoy, then I guess you can add ten points. It's lasagna. Not an engagement ring. Don't get crazy.

Here's the part of the game that really fucks with me. The question-and-answer portion of the Maybe Date. Flirty dude

will ask, "So, you seeing anyone lately?" Obviously, the answer
isn't yes . . . yet. Really, you don't know yet. You *could* be seeing this dude, but the game isn't over yet so we don't know.
If your answer is no, flirty dude will ask why, and asking why
someone is single is an insane question to ask! It's always a
trick! Like I'm really going to answer, "Because I have a rancid
personality! That's why!" So what do you say to the question
of whether or not you're seeing someone? You say, "Lately,
I've been focused on walking in my purpose, you know? I'm
just out here reading books, going to church, and saying *YES*
to life right now." What does it mean? Nothing! But it doesn't
mean *yes* and it doesn't mean *no*. One hundred points for *you*
(*US!*). Then flirty dude will say some stuff about relationships,
and I guess you should listen or whatever, but your appetizer is
probably in front of you by now so don't hesitate to ignore any
warning signs, red flags, or genuinely interesting things flirty
dude might have to say and dive right into that fried calamari.
Then flirty dude will ask how work's going. If you're me, and
I *am* me, this is when you really start paying attention. This is
usually where it all comes together for me. I may humble-brag
my way through how tiring being on the number-one show
in the country is and how it's a lot of work and how, yeah, Ja-
pan was great and I loved it and can't wait to go back but it's
so great to finally sleep in my own bed for once. Whatever
he says after that will determine whether or not this is a date.
What he says next will move us into the lightning round. What
would be great is if his next line was something like "I want
to travel more," "What's your favorite country?" "My favorite
trip was such and such," or whatever, as long as it keeps the
conversation going. Give this guy fifty points! On the flip side,

what usually happens to me is he'll say, "You're busy. I hope you're not too busy to come to Haiti to shoot my documentary," or "I hope you're not too busy to take a look at the pilot I just wrote," or "Wow! I want to go with you! Let me know when you're going again! You can hire me to carry your bags! Whatever I got to do." Even worse is "Damn! Let me know if you need a date for the next award show. I would love to go with you. I can't wait to meet Taraji P. Henson. That's my wife right there! I want to meet celebrities. You're so lucky." Deduct one million points. This is not a date! This is a networking meeting.

I've been on all of these *linkups* over and over, and I've played so many rounds of "Is This a Date?" that I'm paranoid. So, really, I lose the game before I even start to play. I haven't crunched the numbers on how much of that is actually my own fault, but I'd still like to go ahead and place the blame squarely on flirty dude. You smile at me and make me feel like a normal girl even though I have known my entire life that I am not normal. You ask me out and then you try to be *friends* with me. You're nice to me. What the hell is that about? You *know* I'm not normal! What are you doing? I'm a celebrity! Life should be hella dope for me in all ways! Chocolate cake shows up for me when I didn't order it! Why can't someone who's interested in me, not in my career, show up for me, too? Why do all these super-eligible bachelors just want to be my friend? New rule! If you don't want to bone me, you're not allowed to be nice to me. Be super mean to me so that we both know at all times if this is a date or not. I'm sick of playing.

It's clear that I'm more cracked than the Liberty Bell. That's probably the real reason I'm single. The weird part is, I'm fine.

I know I said some things that would make me seem like the opposite of fine, but I'm good. I'm not even lonely. I'm sure you'll read this and begin to see me as a stressed-out woman who spends her Friday nights alone with her twelve cats, researching restaurant menus before going to bed with one of those weird pillows with a man's arm sewn onto it to hug you back. That's weird. I won't deny that I love cats and menus, but that pillow is what nightmares are made of. I usually spend my Friday nights out with my friends. Or I spend them at home writing. Most important, I spend my Friday nights doing whatever I want to do. I know that if I had a boyfriend or, even worse, a husband, I'd spend my Friday nights compromising. I don't think I really want to do that yet. One of my favorite things to do is randomly go on out-of-town trips and not let anyone know where I'm going. I once had a boyfriend who would get mad at me every time I left town but would make no plans to hang out with me when I was around. So I stopped telling him where I'd gone. He found that to be disrespectful. Made me feel like a baller, though. I can be anywhere in the world at any time and it's really only *my* business. I like that kind of freedom. Life *just* got interesting for me. Making big decisions on my own without having to think of some dude's feelings is pretty much my jam right now. I don't miss having a boyfriend most of the time, and I don't care anymore if this is a date or not. I'm just really into walking in my purpose and saying *yes* to life right now. Ya know?

14

ANOTHER PSYCHIC
TOLD ME SO

You should really get into film and television.
— the psychic I saw a month ago

M Y FRIEND CRYSTAL AND I were walking around in
Manhattan. We were in that weird phase when you're
done being a kid but you're not a full adult yet. If we
had a weekend off from college, we were too old to spend it
at an arcade or in Times Square under the window of *Total
Request Live*. (Remember *TRL*? We used to cut class and hang
out there to get a glimpse of pop stars. Obviously, we were
so cool!) But we were too young to have a boozy brunch and
get our nails done. So we window-shopped. This one day, a
woman approached us and touched my arm, stopping us.

"I'm sorry. I know this is weird, but I just had to stop you
and tell you that I see a very bright future for you."

"What?" I asked, confused.

"I'm a psychic and I can see in your eyes that you're going to be a very important person. I don't usually stop people on the street like this, but I just had to tell you that you're really special."

I looked at Crystal. We shared an expression of suspicion and intrigue.

"What?" I was still confused.

"I'm telling you. You're special. You're gonna be famous, girl! Like Oprah! I do psychic readings for a living. I have a shop around the corner. I'd love to give you a reading. I'll do it for you for free." She started to write the address and her number down on a piece of paper. This was exciting but also kind of sketchy. Even then I knew that if something was free I should be suspicious of it. She handed me her information and urged me to come in. I never did. Seemed crazy. I was at the worst stage of my eating disorder, depressed, and pretherapy. In other words, having a pretty bad time in life that year. At that point, I was contemplating not having a future at all. So hearing that something good was going to happen was important. Not that I really believed that psychic. Or Tola, either. Years had gone by since my cowry-shell reading, but there was that word again: *famous*. Let's be clear. I actually don't see any personal value in fame. Life is life, and being famous doesn't make it any easier. When I was a young kid, I thought it might be fun and amazing to be famous because I assumed that fame resulted in a better life. But as a teenager, I realized that Amy Fisher was famous. There are several movies and books about her, and she even has a cool celebrity nickname, the Long Island Lolita. She's totally famous, but not for a good reason: she slept with a married man and then attempted to kill his wife. Monica Lewinsky is someone else whose life was kind of ruined by the bad kind of fame.

Mom is a little famous, with her pretty large following from singing in the subway, and has been for years. This is not the bad kind of fame, to her way of thinking, but it caused me nothing but trouble. When I was out with Mom, people would recognize her and tell her how much they appreciated her voice. Then they would often ask me if I sang like my mom. I hated this question. It felt like pressure to be as amazing as Mom was. I would often say, "I sing better than my mom!" in order to seem . . . precocious? (No points for precocious, but many points for being an awkward yet manipulative weirdo.) Anyway, Mom's always been pretty good at taking a compliment when (and sometimes before) she hears one. I, on the other hand, would panic simply because a stranger was looking and talking to us. "What the fuck, stranger? Can we live? Who even *are* you? Stop talking to us! She's MY mom!" was my inner dialogue. As I grew, so did my panic. I look a lot like Mom, and by the time I was a teenager, I was almost as tall as she was (I'm still not taller. At this point, I'm just waiting for her to shrink. Then *I'll* be the boss!) and we shared the same body type, so when I was on the train or bus by myself, people would sometimes ask me where I was going to perform. They thought I was Mom. Rude, right? She's a smooth thirty years older than I am! I know that black don't crack, but COME ON! So I had to explain to a stranger that I wasn't Mom, and then they'd ask me if I sang, too, and how old I was, and all of a sudden I was trapped in my worst nightmare: SMALL TALK

WITH A STRANGER! AHHHHHH!!!! This is what I thought fame would be like and I preferred not to be famous. Just rich, please and thank you!

Later in the same year that the psychic stopped me on the street, Mom told me that she had met a director who wanted to work with her. A film director named Susan Batson. Ms. Batson happens to also be an actress and a famous acting coach, but Mom had never heard of her. Ms. Batson was at the beginning of adapting the novel *Push* by Sapphire to film, and she wanted Mom to play the role of Mary, a poverty-stricken mother living on welfare. Mary has a daughter, Precious, who she molests and abuses. (I know what you're thinking, *Wait, isn't that* your *role?* and you're right. Just chill. We'll get there, babe.) Mom's a singer, not an actor. Ms. Batson wanted her anyway. She thought Mom would be able to play Mary as a woman with dreams and talent whose life was derailed by the birth of her daughter and who takes her frustrations out on the girl through physical and sexual abuse. Mom hated that idea. She explained to Ms. Batson that she'd been an educator and didn't want the parents of her students to see the movie and think she was capable of doing such a terrible thing. Ms. Batson asked her to read the book first before making up her mind. "So you're going to be a movie star!?" I asked excitedly that day.

"NO! I'm not doing this movie! You know people are crazy! I don't want people to think I'm really like that."

"Are you serious?! It's a movie! No one's going to think you're down with child sexual abuse!"

"No. I don't think I can do this. I'm gonna read the book, but I'm almost sure I won't do this movie."

Dammit, Mom! Didn't she realize that she could be a real-life star? The star she was always meant to be? A day or two later, Mom left for a tour of Spain. She was singing with a choir. Mom read the book while traveling, and when she got back, she came to my room to tell me that she had officially decided to pass on the role. I thought she was insane and I told her so. She handed me the book, and said, "Here. When you read it, you'll see why I don't want to do it."

"Ugh! Fine. You're still crazy though."

"I shouldn't play this role. No one knows me. People might think I'm really like this. I don't need someone trying to fight me in the street for what I do in a movie. It should go to a known actress. Mo'Nique should play this role. People know she's not really like this."

"People aren't *that* crazy, Mom!"

"Just read it. And if you want, I can see if they've cast the daughter yet. Maybe I can get you an audition."

"Pass."

"All right," she said, closing my door and leaving my room. I inhaled that book. I couldn't put it down. It was both a hard and easy read. Precious was a character sadder than I'd ever encountered in either life or fiction. She was also filled with more hope than I personally could ever muster up. I was excited to see this book adapted to film. At this point, I'd like to remind you that I'm being completely honest in this chapter and every chapter in this book. I have an insanely good long-term memory so I remember all of this.

So if I told my mom to make the leap, to play Mary, why'd I say no to the idea of auditioning for the role of Precious? Because it didn't make any fucking sense! I wasn't an actress. I was in school for psychology. That's what I was going to be. A professional in the field of psychology. Sure, I was so depressed that making it there was unlikely, but I digress. Mom was the star. She was the artist. I had suffered through her dreams of stardom enough for two lifetimes. She was talented, but still she and Ahmed and I had slept in a bunk bed for five years. I'd seen Mom's talent and drive but more of her sacrifice and rejection. Dreams are dreams. Reality is something different. Reality is the electricity and cable being cut off for late payments and sleeping in the living room so that your children can each have a room of their own. No, thank you. I wasn't strong or talented enough to dream like Mom did.

Strangely enough, I discovered that I liked acting soon after this. Not that I thought of it as acting at the time. I was staying with Crystal at her mom's house in the Bronx. I think her mom could see that I was on the verge of a breakdown, and she said that I could live with them for the summer. I needed the change of scenery. Crystal was a theater major at Lehman College, and she was in her first play there that summer of 2003. *Peter Pan*. She played an Indian and a pirate. I was bored and sad a lot, so Crystal suggested I come to rehearsals. Seemed like a good way to let the day pass. I became an Indian and a pirate also. It wasn't much, but it was the most fun I'd ever had. Crystal's friends became mine. I was still very sick and depressed, but at least I was around other people. AND there was a bar near the school that didn't card so I discovered booze. That shit is delicious, and it would often help me forget that I was sad! Hooray! (I don't recommend it, but I don't *don't* recommend it.)

The director of *Peter Pan* was super fun but intense. His

name was Guy Ventoliere and he scared the living shit out of me. I didn't know how to act like everyone else in the play. They were in school for theater and I was just killing time. The difference was evident. When the set for the play was built, I immediately broke an entire staircase by hastily jumping off it (seriously). Once during rehearsal, Guy called me out for watching the scene instead of being in it. These are two different things, but I hadn't realized it until Guy told me to get my shit together and be more mindful of my surroundings. When I sang "Pirate Song" with the other actors, Guy called me out again.

"Gabby. Your singing. It's too good." (I know I've already said that my family trait is confidence and big talk, but swear to God, I'm not making this part up!)

"You want me to stop?" I asked, too scared of him to take the compliment.

"No. Make it your own."

"You want me to be louder?" I always thought the answer was to be louder.

"I don't know. Just make it your own."

"I can sing the harmony if you want."

"Yeah! That's great. Do that."

I loved being in that play. I remained very afraid of Guy and very sick, but doing that play for an audience of children was the most important thing I'd ever done. It was a way to fill my life with more than just constant sadness. Dark yo.

After *Peter Pan*, there were auditions for *The Wiz*. All of my new friends were auditioning so I decided to audition, too. It was fall, but by now, I was officially not going to college and enrolled in therapy. Theater became my lifeline. I was cast as

Glinda the Good Witch. Dope. I was having actual fun at night while attending my therapy classes during the day. No one except Crystal knew about this. I am still grateful to her for keeping my sickness under wraps with her friends and also for dealing with my rampant mood swings. I was very hard on her. She was the closest person to me, so I often tried my best to make her feel like shit for the crime of being a normal, blossoming woman. I was often just mad that she wasn't as sad as I was. She was very kind to share her friends, her plays, and her college experience with me. She remains one of the better people I've encountered in my life.

One day while she and I and a few others were waiting for rehearsal to begin, a woman walked over to me. She had walked past us about twice before approaching. None of us knew her.

"Sorry, I just have to tell you something," she said. "You're going to be famous one day."

"What?" I asked. Shit, you'd think I'd be used to it by now, right?

"I'm psychic. I know that sounds crazy, but I am. I don't charge for it or anything, but I can see in your eyes that you have a big future in front of you."

"Oh, no! I'm not a theater major like everyone else. I don't even go here."

"What?" Now she was confused. She apparently hadn't realized that most of the people in that hallway were theater students. "No, this is about you. I saw you when I walked by before and I just *had* to say something. You're really special. One day the entire world will be listening to you."

"What?" (Come on, Gabby! Say something other than "what?"!)

"I see you talking to Oprah. (Oprah? Again?!) You're going to be famous. I see you talking to her."

"What am I famous for?"

"I don't know. I swear I see it in your eyes. Your confidence. It's one of a kind. You're going to write a book. You're going to help people with your confidence."

I had probably just secretly thrown up and fantasized about cutting the fat off my body with a steak knife after a five-hour day of therapy. Bitch, please. What confidence? Where the fuck was it?

"Oh, wow. Okay. Thank you." She left and that was that.

Eventually, I finished my daily therapy classes and started working at the phone sexery. I was becoming an adult: more bills and responsibilities and less time to play make-believe in the Bronx. I was grateful for the friends I'd made there, but soon I wasn't doing any acting or singing at all. Which was fine. It was never the plan to begin with.

After several years working at the phone-hoe station, I was twenty-four years old and plan A, the one where I was going to go to school for psychology, was back in effect. I was finally old enough to get financial aid to pay for my schooling, and I had enrolled at Mercy College. There was a campus on Thirty-fourth Street in Herald Square. The phone-hoe station was on Thirtieth Street, just up the block. By now I had been promoted to monitor, which meant that it was my job to listen in on phone calls to make sure that the talkers were following the rules and that the callers were well taken care of (wink wink). I scheduled my classes around work shifts; I needed about fifteen minutes of travel time in between. THIS was adulthood! I figured that I would cross the bridge of whether being a therapist was actually still my dream when I finally got my degree.

I still thought about performing. That year on my birthday, before I started back at school, Crystal took me to see *Hairspray* on Broadway. It was the best surprise ever! *Hairspray* was one of my favorite movies, but I'd yet to see the stage version. The curtain rose on Tracy Turnblad in her bed. The music began and Tracy opened her eyes and started to sing: "Oh, oh, oh, woke up today feeling the way I always do."

By the end of that one line, I was crying. The song had hardly begun and I was already in tears. Seems I really identified with Tracy, in a body that people are less inclined to accept and respect but still determined to be happy and share her talent. It hit me all at once that I was talented. That I, like Mom, had a gift to offer the world, but that, unlike Mom, I was wasting it. I was smart; I had a voice, a point of view. I could be an artist! I could make art with my life, but instead I was listening to guys jack off over the phone by night and chasing a career I no longer really wanted by day. I hadn't realized that I cared about being an artist until that very moment. I cried until intermission. My instincts had been telling me to pursue something else — art — but my fear had been louder.

Luckily, the universe (or whatever) was stronger than my doubts.

My first week of classes was pretty easy. It was my third college, after all. I had class just about every day. I had to take a language class for my major, and Mercy offered an American Sign Language class. I'd been wanting to learn ASL since I was a child. Mom knew the alphabet and a few words here and there from teaching differently abled kids, and I'd always admired that. I also had a family psychology course that I couldn't wait to sink my teeth into. That first week of school, I got a call from my friend Henry Ovalles. Henry was a Lehman graduate, one of the school's more talented actors who was now the assistant director of Lehman's theater department. He was calling me because he'd learned about a film audition he thought might be right for me. I hadn't been a part of any production in about two years at that point. Henry said he knew that but figured he'd give it a shot: the casting agents were looking for a heavyset black girl between eighteen and twenty-five years old. I asked what the role was.

"The movie is called *Push*. It's based on a book by someone named Sapphire. The audition is for the lead role, Precious. The audition is here at Lehman on Monday," he said deliberately. As if he wasn't blowing my fucking mind!

Mom was out of town doing something that night, but I called her and told her about the *Push* audition resurfacing after almost five years. I asked if the book was still in the house. She told me where to find it and encouraged me to go to the audition. I reread the first page and put it back on the shelf. What was I doing? What did I think was going to happen? I wasn't an actor and I had *just* put my life back on track. I'd survived an almost three-year eating disorder, panic attacks, depression, and failing out of school. I'd found my footing while taking phone sex calls for ten cents a minute just so I could save money to go back to school for the third time. I had my first family psychology class on Monday, and I didn't want to miss it to audition to play an incest survivor. (The irony is not lost on me.) I'd never done an actual audition. College theater was a thing, but was it really? This audition was for a real movie with a director I actually knew and respected! During the five years the book was making its way to production, Lee Daniels, a powerhouse director and producer, had taken over from Susan Batson. At the time, his film *Shadowboxer* was constantly running on Showtime. I'd seen it over and over. The movie has a scene in it featuring Helen Mirren and Cuba Gooding, Jr., having sex while Helen wears a birthday hat. I like shit like that. Anyway, this audition would be the real deal, and I didn't think I was capable of that.

By Monday morning, I still wasn't sure where I was going when I left the house. I put my hair up in a ponytail and dressed like a teenager just in case I ended up at the audition. I also grabbed my books for class. I could either go uptown to the Bronx to audition for this movie role that I was never going to get, or I could go downtown to my class and then straight to work afterward. I walked outside — there was a movie crew filming on the downtown side of the street. (I later heard that it was Denzel Washington's *American Gangster.* I'm not sure that's true but, of course, I'm going to go with it.) I tried to walk through the film set to get to the downtown train station. A production assistant stopped me. He was very friendly. He had a big smile. He smiled that big smile at me and explained that there was filming going on and asked me politely to cross the street. To the uptown side of the street. So I did. Then I figured, since I'm here . . .

When I got to Lehman, I found out that the audition was in the same theater space that *Peter Pan* had been in. If you're

starting to think, *This is unbelievable,* believe it. It all really happened like this. There was a sign-up table with a small pile of
one-page excerpts of the script. I had yet to learn that these
audition sheets are called *sides.* I grabbed one and sat down to
read. Henry walked over with a girl in tow. A heavyset black girl
just like me. I looked at Henry like, *"Really,* homie? I thought
you only called me! You called ALL your fat black girlfriends?
I *see!"* but I didn't say it. He said he was glad I could make the
audition, and he wished me and this new girl I'd never met before luck. Then he left. The new girl (I don't remember getting her name, but I sometimes call her Sabourey Gidibe in my
private thoughts) asked what role I was auditioning for. As if
she didn't know. I told her the same one she was. She might've
mentioned something about being nervous. I wasn't nervous
in the least. I was disappointed in myself for missing my first
family psych class and wasting my time. I waited about five
minutes, and then I was called into the theater to audition. I
was asked to sit in a chair opposite a camera and casting directors Jessica Kelly and Billy Hopkins, who himself had launched
the careers of countless actors and cast *Good Will Hunting,*
American Psycho, Se7en, and my personal favorite, *Uncle Buck.*
I sat across from the two of them and I wasn't nervous. This
was magic. I'm *always* nervous. I'm nervous right now! (To
be fair, I'm alone at my cousin's house in LA, it's after eleven
at night, and I think I hear a coyote howling in the distance!
I'm about to call 911!) But I wasn't nervous in front of them.
The scene I auditioned was Precious meeting with a therapist
and telling her how depressing her life with her mother was.
(Again, the irony is not lost on me.) When I was done, Billy
and Jessica were quiet before finally saying, "Wow! That was

great!" I, of course, didn't believe them, and Billy said something like "Trust me, that was really good!" I got up to leave, and they handed me some longer sides to memorize and told me they would give me a call soon for a second audition. On the way out, I wished good luck to Sabourey Gidibe and told her it was cool and there was nothing to be nervous about. Then I got on the subway and headed down to the phone sexery. I was going to be early for my shift as a monitor, but the phones were busy as usual so I jumped on the talker floor and picked up a few calls to make some extra money. By the time I left the talker floor less than an hour later, I had a voice mail from Billy Hopkins inviting me to the callback audition the next day. Still, I wasn't feeling much. It was almost as if it was a regular Monday.

By the next morning, I had memorized both scenes I'd been given — the same one with the therapist from the day before along with another one where Precious is telling her class that she has contracted HIV from her father. Mad emotional yo. I asked Mom to read the scene with me. I hadn't attempted to cry on cue while rehearsing the scene by myself. I hadn't even said the words aloud up until then, but as I read with Mom, when it was time to cry, I just did. Mom was crying, too. Pussy. She asked if I wanted to go over it again and I said no, I wanted the emotion to feel new for the audition. I don't know where that idea came from. All of a sudden, after being on autopilot for years, I was making real decisions.

At the callback audition, this time at some office way downtown in Tribeca, there weren't any other actresses who looked like me. No Sabourey Gidibes waiting for their lives to change. Just me. Jessica came out to greet me. She told me how impressed they'd been with my audition the day before. I think I said okay instead of thank you. It sounded like I was being a sarcastic asshole, but I think I was just trying to process everything. In fact, I figured they were lying to me when they said I was good. I was a loser who had flunked out of school for being sad. I was a phone sex worker who lived with my mother. All of a sudden I was in the casting office of the guy who had discovered Macaulay Culkin. Seriously, what the fuck? Finally, I was ushered into the audition room where Billy was waiting. I think there was a reader and casting assistant in the room as well. I fumbled a word on my first take — I was finally feeling a tiny bit nervous — but then I must've remembered that this was all a complete waste of time and my nerves went away. I cried when the script told me to cry, and I delivered the scene as if I were completely out of my body. I don't know who I was on that day (perhaps the *real* Sabourey Gidibe). When I was done, Billy and Jessica stared at me for a few seconds as I waited for it to be over.

Then Billy quickly demanded, "Get her a script. Get her a script!" The casting assistant rushed to get me a full script. Not just the sides. I stood up to leave and asked what was going to happen next.

"We'll call you. You're going to audition for Lee!"

"This whole thing?" I asked, referring to the script. If they didn't know that they were working with a novice, they knew now.

"No! You're just going to do this same audition again with the director. We'll call you!" Billy said.

I listened to the *Hairspray* soundtrack on my headset on the way back home on the subway. By the time I got out of the train station, about half an hour later, I had a voice message from Lee Daniels's office. He wanted to meet me the next day. This was almost starting to seem normal for me and the subway.

I went to class the morning of the audition and asked someone to switch shifts with me at work so I could make the four o'clock appointment. I had read the entire script and brought it along with me in case Lee planned to point to a random scene and make me deliver it. Not that I could memorize it that quickly or that Lee would be that sadistic. I was just ready for anything. I got to Lee's office way too early. I waited in front of the building and used the extra time I had to pray. I didn't pray that I would get the role. I prayed that whatever my life was supposed to be, whatever my path was, I would finally be on it. I was only twenty-four years old, but I was tired of fear. I was tired of running away from something I could see into something I couldn't. I didn't know why this book, these characters, this production had shown up in my mother's life five years before or why they were showing up in mine now, but I knew this was my purpose. It wasn't that my purpose was to be a movie star; it was just for my life to begin. (I also decided that if I didn't get the role of Precious I would never see the movie and I'd curse the girl who actually got the role. Curses to you, Sabourey Gidibe!)

At 3:50, I went upstairs to Lee's office. He wasn't there yet. I sat and waited for him. A few minutes after four, Lee walked in. He was over six feet tall with hair that scraped the ceiling. He was holding plastic bags in both hands.

"Guys, I have cake! I brought back cake from Brooklyn!"

he announced. "Pineapple upside-down cake! Anybody want some cake?"

It was like a fairy tale! He was exactly what I thought he'd be and he had cake! I was soon sitting across from him at his desk. Behind him on the wall were headshots of the actors already cast in the film. There she was. Mo'Nique's picture was on the wall. Mo'Nique was playing the mother. The same role Mom had turned down, saying Mo'Nique should play it. Typical. Yet Mom won't say on record that she's psychic.

Lee offered me some cake, but in my new tradition of going against my instincts, I declined. He asked if I'd ever acted before. I told him about *Peter Pan* and Glinda the Good Witch. He remarked in a kind voice that he was very impressed with my audition. I held on tightly to the script in my hand. I was sure he was just seconds away from asking me to deliver a scene. He asked me if I was in school. I said I was. He asked what I would do if I got the role.

I said, "Something would have to give. The opportunity to be in a movie doesn't come along every day."

We kept talking. I was losing my patience. I just wanted to get this last audition over with. All of the idle chitchat was making me nervous. Lee finally said, "You're really smart." Oh, great! Another person thinks I'm smart! Can I stop listening to guys beg me to make them wear panties over the phone now?

"Thank you."

"I want you to be in my movie."

"As what?" I asked, never one to believe a stranger wanted to do anything but hurt me. (I gotta stop that shit.)

"As Precious," he said. It was quiet. I think. I also could've been screaming. I'm not sure. I had auditioned on Monday and now it was only Wednesday and the prophecy of fame was finally being fulfilled. I was going to be a movie star. It couldn't have been that easy but it was. *Now* I was nervous. I cried like a little girl, and Lee grabbed my hand and walked me around the production office and introduced me to everyone by saying, "This is Gabby! She's our Precious!"

That night, Lee drove me home. On the way, he asked if I had a boyfriend.

"No, but now that I'm going to be a movie star, I'm gonna get pregnant by a basketball player and lock down that child support," I answered. He laughed hysterically.

He had asked me earlier in the day in his office what I did for a living. Since by then I had already gotten the part, and I had also seen *Shadowboxer* enough times to know that he would think my being a phone sex operator was a riot, I told him. Now in the car he wanted to know about my most disgusting callers. I shared stories of men who called to be abused by dominant women who would force them to be with black men with huge dicks. He laughed and laughed, and said, "We won't tell Oprah that story."

"You think I'll get to do *Oprah*?" I asked, excitedly.

"Of course you will! Oprah will live for you!"

He asked if I'd ever read the book *Push*. I told him that I had and that my mother had given it to me when she was asked years ago to audition for the role of Mary. He was surprised and asked who my mother was. I explained that she wasn't an actor and that he wouldn't know her unless he takes the subway a lot.

"Wait a minute! Is your mother a singer? Is she the one who sings all the Whitney Houston songs?" he asked.

"Yeah. That's my mom."

"That's your MOM? Honey, she's EVERYTHING! I wanted her for this movie! I wanted her for Mary! That was years ago! You are her daughter?" He couldn't believe it. Neither could I, really.

We started shooting three weeks later. Filming lasted about three and a half months. It wasn't until the last day that I learned how many girls had auditioned for the role of Precious. Around four hundred, I'm told. There was even an acting summer camp where they put about twenty plus-size black girls in a house together, and every week there were auditions, and every week a girl was cut and sent home. It was like *American Idol* or something. Apparently, there's footage of this Precious Camp, but I've never seen it. At the end of summer, the production was down to two girls, but they still weren't sure they'd found Precious yet. (So many Sabourey Gidibes and still no Gabourey Sidibe!) That's when they held the last open casting calls and found me. I had no idea how many things had to go wrong for me to win that role, but I decided by then to stop paying attention to what might have gone wrong and start being grateful for all the things that had gone right instead. A year and a half later, Oprah saw the film before it was released and, along with Tyler Perry, came aboard as a producer. Oprah asked me to be on her show, but first she wanted a camera crew to follow me around for a day. I insisted that the *Oprah* crew follow me down to the subway to see Mom perform. I was determined to get footage of her subway performance on *Oprah*. My one and only appearance on *Oprah* happened to be the show when she announced her retirement. I had made it just in time for all of the psychics to be right. I cried like a bitch throughout the entire show. Emotions yo!

How many psychics does it take to convince a sad little girl that she can be much more than the world is telling her she is? None. She's got to be able to convince herself to show up for her own life. I still don't see any real value in fame. Sure, I skip most lines. I get plenty of free clothes and jewelry, and at restaurants, as we've seen, the chef sends out free desserts. But fame isn't what gets me out of bed in the morning. It's purpose. I've found my purpose and this is it. I love what I do. I'm grateful to be a two-time college dropout who finally believes in psychics. I'm not recommending it, but I'm not *not* recommending it.

15

HEAD OF HOUSEHOLD

I'm a girl in a world in which my only
job is to marry rich.

— Angelica Schuyler (*Hamilton*)

WAS TALKING TO THIS GUY I know about how he grew up in a poor family. I didn't know him that well and he was also really handsome, so I immediately turned the conversation into a competition. This is how I deal with handsome men I'd like to bone. I become aggressively weird and freak them out. That's my move. Anyway, he said, "My family was really poor. *Really* poor!" I, having played the "my family's so poor we can't afford to pay attention" game many times in my life, countered with "Oh, yeah? Your family ever wait in line for government cheese?" Then I smiled as though that memory were a shiny trophy. He made a noise like *duh!* and rolled his eyes. "Of course, man! We were *severely* poor." He rolled his eyes at me and called me "man"? Clearly, he was into me, but

I also realized that I was losing this poor-off. My parents were poor, but I don't think I would've categorized us as "severely poor." My only choice was to become even more aggressive. "Oh, God. What? Did your family have to live in a fucking car or something?" With his face showing the appropriate amount of distaste for what I'd so flippantly asked, he answered, "Actually, we stayed in a shelter." That's it. I was officially beat. My family has never stayed in a shelter. I thought about bringing up the BCW and foster-home business, but that wouldn't have lent anything to the argument. I thought about bringing up having to use food stamps, but shelter beats food stamps. I didn't know what to say because I'd asked a terrible question and forced a terribly personal and sad answer out of someone I barely knew. So I doubled down on my invasiveness. "Whoa! What was that like?" Why won't I stop asking questions? He told me about how for Christmas college kids would come to the shelter and hand out toys and candy and stuff. That it was the best day ever. He said that he decided as a kid that when he was an adult and had money he would do the same as those college kids. He'd buy toys and give them out at homeless shelters. I asked if he'd kept his word. He said that he did and still does. I was slain. He won at being poorer than I had been and he won at being a better person than I was. Game over.

My family was poor when I was growing up. Just not *shelter* poor. But I spent the bulk of my childhood in fear that neither of my parents could afford to raise me.

As an adult, I know I fucked up my childhood. I see I didn't have to worry about not having enough money. I wish I could have learned from Biggie. He said, "Mo money, mo prob-

lems." And I had none when I was a kid. That means no problems, right?

For *Precious,* I didn't yet have a manager. Because it was my
first acting job, I made scale, about $2,500 a week. A month af-
ter we started shooting, I still hadn't received a check. Other
people were getting their paychecks on set, and I asked where
mine was. The production manager said it was at the office
and wanted to know if I could wait for it until the following
week. My bank account had a negative balance of more than
a hundred dollars. I asked the production manager to send
someone to get the check for me immediately. A part of me
was afraid that I'd be called a bitch. Another part of me was
proud for having demanded to be paid on time for all of the
work I'd been doing. Sixteen-hour days for weeks and I was
broke! I was in the hair-and-makeup trailer when the check arrived. Lee Daniels and the film's producer, Sarah Siegel-Mag-
ness, came in and said, "Gabby, we have something for you."
Sarah was recording us on her iPhone. Lee handed me my first
film check, and Sarah screamed, "You're rich now, baby!" I
opened the envelope, and said, "Oh, cool. Thanks." The check
was for $2,500. I most certainly was NOT rich now, and it sur-
prised me that they thought I would be super excited to have
worked that hard for so little money. Was it the largest check
I'd ever seen with my name on it? YES! But I'd made $1,600 on
my best week down at the phone sexery, which was a steady
job. I wasn't able to see that film check as being part of a bigger picture. All I could think about was how the shoot would
be over soon and that more than likely I wouldn't be able to

get another acting job until the film came out in a year or so. What was I supposed to do until then? Hoard and worry. The starry-eyed girl I was supposed to be when I opened my first film check that day in the trailer was already dead.

When the filming was done, I had made a bit more than $30,000 before taxes. I think. Coupled with the income I'd made as a phone sex operator for the bulk of the year, I had earned more than $50K. My mother and I got our taxes done at the same office, and our tax guy announced to us both that I was now the "head of household." I had made more than double what my mom had. *Head of household* was not a term I'd heard before. I didn't like it. My mom was still a subway singer, and I was now the star of a movie who'd had a steady job in addition for most of the year. I should've seen it coming, but I was faced with the same feeling I had when I was told that the light bill was in my name. Too much responsibility! What's more, I felt guilty for having outearned my mother, an official adult in my eyes. I was just some dumb phone-hoe child who had tripped and fallen into a starring film role. Later that year, while still waiting for *Precious* to be released, I was bored and broke enough to want to get a job. After shooting, I didn't go back to phone sex—while I was away filming, the company had gone out of business. Also, yeah, right! Like I'm going to go from shooting a movie back to pretending to slap myself in the face while some guy pretends he's ejaculating on double D tits. I was officially too fancy for that. (You are, too, by the way. But if they're your tits and you're into it, do your thang, boo.) My mom said that I could go back to school or just hang out while waiting for the release. She said she'd take care of the bills for me; I think she thought that once I was rich and famous I would pay her back in spades. But I handled my bills and portion of the rent with that $50K. It was going fast. Though I had made $50K, I really had only about $10K in my bank account.

Months after *Precious* premiered at the Sundance Film Festival but months before it would premiere to the world, I was experiencing fame without being rich. That's got to be the worst thing ever! I started to get invited to premieres and parties, but I had no fancy clothes to wear, no hair or makeup artist to help, no cute clutch purses for the red carpets. And no limo — I was taking a train or bus to every event. None of that was going to stop me from going, though. The first big Hollywood premiere I was officially invited to was Tyler Perry's *Madea Goes to Jail*. Fancy! Tyler Perry had just signed on as executive producer of *Precious,* which meant I'd be meeting Tyler Perry *and* Oprah! The premiere was at the Loews Theater at Lincoln Center, which had been on my bus route between home and school. Plenty of times I'd pressed my nose up against the window to see if I could see any stars. Now I was going to be a part of the party!

The morning of the premiere I woke up to a commotion in the living room. My mother opened my bedroom door in tears. There were two men in our apartment, the front door was wide open, and they were attaching some sort of notice to it. We were being evicted! Ahmed was looking over some court document, and my mom was crying hysterically and telling the men it was a mistake and begging them to not do this to us and begging me to do something. Me. Everything was moving slowly but very fast at the same time. Me?

My mom doesn't cry much. She's generally collected, level-

headed. I've been the crier in the family. I was always too sensitive. Easily hurt and always afraid of everything. A catastrophic
thinker. Sometimes my mom would quote a children's song
to me: "It's all right to cry. Crying takes the sad out of you."
But mostly she would encourage me to stop, to get over my
feelings. In this moment she was panic-stricken and looking
to me to be the adult. I wasn't crying, but I was far from being the rational parent my mother suddenly needed me to be.
"Gabourey, call Lee! Call Sarah!" She wanted me to call my
rich friends. These were the last people I'd call. But for some
reason she was looking for me to call them so that they could
provide . . . advice? Money? A better apartment to be evicted
from, maybe? I wasn't sure, but I wanted her to stop crying. I
wanted these men to stop evicting us. I felt terrible for not yet
being the kind of rich and famous actress who could afford to
buy my family a mansion we wouldn't be evicted from. With
my mom in hysterics, her face wet with tears, begging me to
call my rich friends, I just did what she asked. I was head of
household, after all.

Sarah and her husband, Gary, both producers of *Precious*,
lived in Denver. While I was waiting around for the film release, Sarah would often fly me out to Denver to spend time
with her and her family, and spoil me with gifts. She never
wrote me a check and I never asked her to, but she and Gary
were very sweet to me. I was also the lead actor in their film.
I was a business expense and an investment. *Precious* would
eventually make millions of dollars for the producers. Our
relationship was personal and it was business. I wasn't naïve
about that. Even as I dialed, I still didn't know what the use of

calling was except to embarrass the shit out of me. I couldn't ask Sarah to pay my family's rent. I never would. Accepting a laptop from her as a birthday gift was one thing, but asking her to support my grown-ass family was out of the question. On top of that, not paying the rent wasn't even what was having us evicted. It turned out to be a clerical error; a check wouldn't have fixed that. But my mom was still crying, and I had a premiere to go to that night. I was going to meet Tyler Perry and Oprah.

I left a message. Maybe I was crying by then. I don't know. I packed my dress for the premiere in a bag along with shoes and a brush for my hair. I was going to go get my hair done with my friend Crystal that day, so I called and asked her if I could spend the night at her house after the premiere that she was not invited to.

In a few minutes Sarah called me back. Our conversation was short and quiet. I wasn't crying.

"Gabby . . . what's going on over there?"

"*Um* . . . something happened. We're being evicted."

"Why? How much is your rent?"

"I . . . no. It's not that."

"What is it?"

". . ."

"Did you tell Lee?"

"No . . . I don't know why I called you . . . We're going to that premiere later."

"Gabby. You have to tell Lee."

". . ."

"Gabby. What do you need from me?"

"I don't know. Nothing. My mom just won't stop crying. She asked me to call you. I don't know what you can do! It's not even money! I don't know what's happening!"

"Gabby. You have to get out of there!"

"I know! The man said an hour!"

"Do you need a hotel?"

"No. I'm going to my friend's house. I have to go."

I hung up. A few minutes later as we were all about to leave the house, Lee called. Talking to Sarah was one thing; she was my friend. Lee still felt like the Wizard of Oz except I couldn't ask him for anything. I wouldn't even know what to ask. I didn't want him to know that my family was being evicted, but he knew. I was ashamed. Our conversation was shorter and even quieter than the one with Sarah.

"Gabby?"

". . ."

"Gabby."

". . . Yeah?" (Now I was crying.)

"What's happening?"

"*Um* . . . we're kinda being evicted?"

"Precious . . . What happened to all of your money?"

"It's complicated. I don't know why I called Sarah. My mom! She has to go to court. I don't know."

Neither of these conversations accomplished whatever my mother thought they should have, if she even knew what that was herself. I was disappointed and angry at her for letting this happen to us. Maybe the clerical error wasn't her fault, but it was her fault that . . . rationally speaking, I wasn't sure why I was mad at her, what to blame her for. So I turned the anger on myself. Here was my chance to save my family from poverty, and I wasn't *ready* to be the hero. I was twenty-four years old, and I'd made more money than my mom that year, but it didn't matter. I couldn't stand up with my family standing on my shoulders. I wasn't ready for head of household.

Later that night I went to the premiere. I don't remember if I had fun. I must have. When I saw Lee, I tried to suppress my embarrassment. I tried to avoid the pity in his eyes and declined his offer to let me stay at his apartment. Besides that, it was a pretty normal night. I mean if normal was to be at a Hollywood premiere broke. That night I slept on Crystal's couch and the morning after the clerical problem was fixed and my family was allowed back into our apartment. Four months later, I got a day job and moved out.

Moving out on my own felt like a step toward becoming a successful adult. I thought my leaving would be great for my tiny three-person family. Mom would have more room and wouldn't have to worry about providing me with food or anything else. Ahmed would see me surviving and figure out how to be his own version of an adult. He'd pick up the slack and start helping my mom with the rent and bills the way I had. Maybe he'd move out soon after me, and then Mom could move into a one-bedroom apartment in a nicer neighborhood. Maybe I'd soon make enough money to be able to make sure they lived better. I wanted to let Mom know that even though I was leaving I would still be a part of the family. I wouldn't forget about them. I left my checkbook with her and told her that if she needed any help, if she needed money for any reason, she could call me and I'd come over and we'd talk about it and I'd write her a check. What could possibly go wrong?

● ● ●

I am not rich. I can afford my life, but not really anyone else's. I have friends who think I can. Who say, when I ask what they want to do for their birthday, "You can pay my credit card debt for me." And then there's my family. I love the shit outta my family. When I started making more than phone-hoe money, I really wanted to help them as much as I could. I wanted to alleviate their financial fears as much as possible. At first, I would write both Mom and Dad checks whenever they needed them. I gave them gifts and treated them to dinners out. I sent them home in cabs and limos. I bought furniture and replaced broken appliances in their homes, and more times than I can count, I paid their rent. I paid their rent before paying my own. Sometimes I couldn't afford to pay both, but my guilt wouldn't let me pay mine without paying theirs. So I'd just pay theirs. They got used to this. *Really* used to it. My family started to call me less often, but when they did, the conversations ended with "Look. I need . . ." Certain family members *began* the call with "Look. I need . . ." I felt like an ATM machine, not family. Cousins I loved but didn't often talk to would text me to ask for thousands of dollars to help save their house from foreclosure. Mom was featured on the show *America's Got Talent,* and when it turned out she didn't crack the top ten performers and was voted off the show, she didn't go back to singing in the subway. She had a manager now and was putting a band together for her to perform with at talent showcases so people would hire her to sing in different venues around the world. All that cost money; and I was also paying for her to get her nails done; I was helping her buy makeup and wigs. Ahmed needed to borrow money to become a cabdriver (I don't fucking know why!). Dad was truly relentless. He constantly asked me to invest in businesses, asked me to pay for his divorce from Tola, the woman he'd married behind my mother's back (the fucking audacity, right?!). An aunt asked me to move her from Georgia to New York City and buy her nice wigs. All of a sudden I was reduced to how much money I could give out. Even if family members asked if they could "borrow" money, I knew that none of them would ever pay it back. I actually had more respect for the ones who just straight up asked for the money without bothering to convince me that I'd someday see it returned. Either way, no one has paid me back. Ever. No one was even nicer to me after spending my money. Wouldn't it be nice if money bought love? But it doesn't. It buys resentment.

I called my mom once to complain about my aunt asking me to move her across the country and buy her wigs. I was all like, "Why would she think it's appropriate to ask me for *that* much money?!" Mom said, "The family knows how much money you have. We know you have two million dollars. Google said so." I was floored. I had never thought to google how much money I had. I had never considered that Mom would. Or that *anyone* in my family would. Also, Google needs to mind her damn business! My family thought I was a millionaire because I had (maybe!) *earned* two million dollars (like in my lifetime, by the age of thirty!), and for some reason they thought I had that money just lying around. Like maybe I was diving into a vault of it like Scrooge McDuck and that I was so rich the laws of taxation and expenses didn't apply to me!

My family thinks that I have more money than I actually have, and they think I make my living by pretending to jog after Lucious Lyon to tell him that Hakeem fell down a well. By pretending to cast spells and giving Kathy Bates's head the business for being racist. By being super cute and a little bit drunk on nightly talk shows. My career — which I am working harder at than my family could ever imagine — doesn't seem real to cabdrivers and certainly not to my family.

Money changes people. It changed the way my family saw me. It changed how they interacted with me. Perhaps more than it changed them, it changed how I saw them as well. When I was a kid, no one wanted anything from me. Mom didn't need my help. When I became head of household, she realized that she could lean on me in a crisis. When that crisis came the first time, I was unable to be the savior, but every time after, I've been the hero. Moving out has made me a real adult. I'm head of my own household now but not done being the head of theirs. I continue to receive tearful calls from Mom. "We're being evicted." These evictions are not the result of clerical issues anymore. I don't know what it's about anymore. I just write the check and emptily threaten that it's the last time. Somehow, with all the gifts, dinners, and the left-behind checkbook, I've handicapped my family. They have jobs and careers, but I don't know what they would do if I stopped helping them. When we were all poor, we were on the *Titanic* together, but now that I'm no longer poor, I'm on a lifeboat to safety and my family is still sinking. I couldn't have imagined the responsibility of trying to pull them to safety with me. I couldn't have imagined how much it would hurt my back to try to pull them or that it would last forever. One of my famous friends has a family just as expensive as mine. Every time I get those pitiful money calls, I complain to him and swear that I'm not going to write the check this time. That they'll just have to sink or swim. Each time my friend listens, and then says, "You can be mad all you want, but then you'll feel guilty and you'll write the check and then complain some more. Why don't you just save us both some time and write the damn check? Accept your fate." I grumble and then I write the check. I don't know if I can trust that my family can swim anymore, and I could never actually bear to watch them sink.

I'm afraid I'll be getting calls about evictions until my tiny family is gone. Then I'd pay any amount of money just to have them back. Don't you just hate it when rich people complain?

16

SENEGALESE CROWN

*I truly look at edges and natural hairstyles like
dudes look at booties. I just took off my sunglasses
and rolled down the window for a braided bun.*

— my Twitter

S O, AFTER READING THOSE COMMENTS about my
brown/blonde braids, I flew into a fit of rage and pulled
them out. I'll deal with my anger issues later. I found
someone to come to my house to give me black braids to
match my natural color in time for some Washington, D.C.,
events a few days away. But in the meantime, I had to go buy
the new hair, run to two appointments, and get to CVS. I was
on my way to my closet for scarves or a hat to cover my real
hair before heading out for my errands when I passed by my
mirror and saw my reflection. My natural hair was unkempt,
all over the place, and beautiful. *Today's the day,* I thought. *Today's the day for an Afro.* Maybe it was because I knew that later

that day my hair would be in braids so no one would have time to hate my Afro and comment on how terrible it was. Maybe I was sick of thinking about the comments. Maybe I'd spent entirely too much time worrying about what other people think about the hair that grows out of my head. Maybe after years of braids turning into dreads, perms making it fall out, bleach, peroxide, chlorine, and my pigeonholing it into the same weaved style, my hair deserved to live freely! I combed my hair up and out, and put a headband on. Then I left the house.

Part of me felt exposed. Like I wasn't wearing any clothes. Another part of me felt free and confident. Like I wasn't wearing any clothes, but I had great tits and a rocking ass. I felt great! More confident than fearful. No one was pointing and laughing! There were no boos coming from anyone I saw that day. No one said anything at all. By the time I got home, I was feeling pretty good about myself. I felt cute and confident and like I'd finally found my way into the Black Woman Hair Universe of Possibilities. Finally! But then I remembered the Internet. Of course no one had said anything nasty about my hair to my face. Of course no one booed me in person. I live in a polite society of people who usually know better than to comment on another person's appearance to her face. They'd make their comments on the Internet, where they can hide behind their screen names and Twitter handles! If I was really going to wear my Afro proudly, I'd have to post a picture of it to my Instagram account.

I must've taken four hundred selfies before finally settling on the perfect picture to upload. Then, just as I began to post it, I deleted it, put on a new lipstick, and took four hundred more selfies. I was nervous. I was thinking too much. I was taking this too seriously. Finally, after psyching myself up, I posted the picture to Instagram, put my phone in my fridge, and walked away from it for a while. An hour later, I went back to the phone to check the damage. People loved my hair! They thought it looked healthy and beautiful. *Well, shit.* That's what I thought. As nice as it is to get validation from strangers online, I hated that I needed it. I was proud of my hair before I posted it. Why did I need 7,000 people to like it? The hair belongs to me. It's my head. I mean, thanks, Instagram fans, but if I don't like my hair on my own, it's not worth having in the first place. I had several days before my D.C. events, and in the meantime, I was going to wear the hair I wanted.

Three days later I boarded a plane to Washington to join the Creative Coalition and a group of actors and musicians in lobbying for arts education in schools. We were going to be split up into groups and take meetings at the Senate and White House. I'd been invited by the Hearst Corporation and *Cosmopolitan* magazine for the following evening to the White House Correspondents' Dinner.

My hair was braided into a black Senegalese twist. For all of my meetings on Capitol Hill, my hair hung down to my shoulders. I ran my fingers through it whenever I wanted to and tucked it behind my ears. I didn't think about a frame for my face. I felt pretty and confident. The next night, as I stepped into the Correspondents' Dinner, it had started to rain, but I didn't worry about my hair. It wasn't going to move an inch. It was braided and twisted into a high bun with a gold band around it and hid about three hundred bobby pins. My hair perfectly matched the regalness of my custom-made black and gold ball gown. My hair was perfect. It was exactly what I wanted it to be. I wore my hair like a crown. The little girl I used to be with braids and a baby doll strapped to her back was proud. That same girl who sat on sofa pillows between her mother's legs enduring the pain of hair tugging and pulling was proud as well. I floated around that party like Cinderella before midnight.

As we were making our way through the party, people began to stop me to ask for pictures, and I got separated from my group pretty quickly. Eventually, I got really hot and sweaty. While my hair wasn't a problem, my heels and huge dress were quite cumbersome to maneuver while posing for pictures. I went into a room and saw a sofa to sit on so I could blot away the sweat and reapply makeup. Just then, a woman came over to me, and said, "I work for the president of the United States and the first lady. They want to invite you to a private reception before the dinner starts." Holy shit. I was going to meet President Barack Obama and First Lady Michelle Obama! I began to sweat even more. The woman led me to the entrance to the reception room, where I had to walk through a metal detector. No biggie. I've been to high school. I know my way around a metal detector. Now I was in the room where many people were standing in line to meet POTUS and FLOTUS. I wasn't ready. I rushed to the bathroom and stood in front of the mirror blotting the sweat from my face. A few women in ball gowns came in. I blurted out that I was about to meet the president and that I couldn't stop sweating. The ladies assured me that everything would be fine and that I should take as much time as I needed. I listened to them and waited until I was calm. By the time I joined the line, though, I was sweating profusely again. Luckily, the line was long and ran along a bar. I just kept asking for ice water. I must've drunk a bathtub full of ice water to try to calm down, but it wasn't working.

Somehow in that crowded room and confusing line, I ended up standing next to this beautiful black woman. I could tell she was African. Her hair was in a beautiful Senegalese twist like mine. We introduced ourselves and she asked for a picture. I took it and asked where she was from. She told me she was from the Congo. I blurted out that I loved her hair and that I was always struggling with what to do with my own hair and that I was proud and so happy to be meeting the president while wearing a hairstyle that was representative of my culture, my father's country, and the birthplace of civilization. I blurted out that I was so happy to be both African and American while meeting our nation's first African American leader whose own African roots were so clearly displayed in his name. Like mine. Somewhere in my blurting out what must've sounded like high-pitched nonsense to this stranger, I forgot to be nervous. I forgot to sweat myself into a river. All of the rest had drifted away and all that was left was pride.

After just a few more minutes, I was next in line to greet the leader of the free world and the first lady. I had a slip of paper in my hand with my name printed on it that I'd been given at the metal detector line. The paper was to be given to a woman so she could announce my name to the president and first lady. When the woman began to say my name, President Obama cut her off, and said, "I know who she is! You're the BOMB, girl!" He stretched his arms wide and embraced me with a hug and a kiss on the cheek. Yeah . . . the president of the United States of America said that I was the "bomb"! That's pretty much the end of the story. I mean, what else do you need to know? The president said I was the "BOMB"! Good night.

17

WILL I STILL BE BEAUTIFUL WHEN I'M NOT FAT?

True life: I can't stop checking out my ass in the mirror . . . and the window . . . and in shiny cars I pass in the street.

— my Twitter

HAD MOSTLY BEEN ASLEEP DURING my two-night hospital stay. I've always had trouble sleeping, but the anesthesia stayed in my body for so long after surgery that it was hard to keep my eyes open long enough for the nurses to check my vitals and force me to walk around the hospital floor every four hours. Right after one of my hospital strolls, I lay back in that weirdly comfortable hospital bed and scrolled through my phone to see what amazing shit on the Internet I had been missing during my slumber. My birthday was three days before the surgery, so my phone was filled with belated birthday texts, calls, and tweets. I scrolled down my Instagram and came across a comment.

"I don't understand why you still fat. All that fame and money and you ain't got no trainers or surgery? The fuck!"

I smiled. Then I laughed. I laughed so hard I was afraid I would pop my brand-new stomach. I held on to it as I continued to laugh, hoping I wouldn't hurt myself. I clicked that little button the nurses kept telling me to click when I felt pain. They said it was morphine or something, but I'm sure it was just a placebo, like the walk button at pedestrian crosswalks. The button makes you think you can control something, but really, you ain't got the juice like that. I pressed the "morphine" button anyway and continued laughing like it was my last laugh ever. The entire bed and even the IV bag stand that looked like a robotic coat hanger were vibrating. Maybe the little button *did* work and I was totally high, because I couldn't stop laughing at that comment. All I could think was that in a few months when I've decided the time is right to start talking about my surgery that asshole is going to claim it was all his idea! He'll probably tell his friends, "I TOLD her to do it! I wrote it on an Instagram picture of her as a bunny! I TOLD HER!" This guy and all the other Internet commenters who have tried to shame me into changing my body are going to think they finally got through to me, that they have some power over what I do with my body. But that's the funny thing about Internet comments. They are the same as those walk buttons. Just placebos. They don't really have any power over me. You ain't got the juice like that!

Surgery is a huge deal. HUGE! I'd never been anesthetized before. I'd never spent the night in a hospital. The closest was when I went to the emergency room years ago for my tonsils.

They are huge all the time, but if I have a bad cold in the winter, they swell up even more and rub up against each other. I waited patiently but uncomfortably in the middle of the night at Harlem Hospital Center as gunshot victim after gunshot victim kept coming in and trumping my petty little problem of not being able to breathe. I totally get it. (Harlem Hospital Center is *great* with gunshot wounds, by the way ... in case you need to know that.) But I had a phone sex shift in the morning, and all of a sudden it was after 3 a.m. and I started to have a panic attack about missing work, which made my breathing worse, so I gestured for the closest nurse. She took a second to look in my mouth with a flashlight and a popsicle stick. "Oh, God! Your tonsils are touching!" "Das what I was tellin' you befo!" I screamed, with the popsicle stick still on my tongue. She placed me in a room by myself, and the next thing I knew, I woke up with an IV in my arm. It was three hours later, but my tonsils had shrunk and I was free to go to work. You are thinking, *Why didn't she get her tonsils removed?* Because I couldn't get tonsil surgery and sit around eating popsicles and Jell-O all day in between phone sex calls! That's crazy! YOU'RE crazy! Also, the idea of being put to sleep and ripped open *while* I slept seemed insane. Either way, that was the most dramatic hospital experience I've ever had.

I've read somewhere that the average adult American has no less than five medical conditions at any given time. I suppose I'm not different. I have high blood pressure, high cholesterol, low *good* cholesterol, anemia, and I'm constantly treading the line between diabetic and prediabetic. Diabetes isn't necessarily a condition I am afraid of. I was a small child when Dad was diagnosed. I know it's hereditary. I always knew I'd be a fat adult, so I saw diabetes in my future one way or the other. For a long time, I was too busy, too unfocused, too hungry, and too filled with excuses to do anything about it. The first time my doctor called me to let me know that I was straight-up diabetic, I wasn't surprised, but I still felt really stupid. I could've been going to my trainer who was on standby, ready to work with me whenever I was available. I'd seen countless dieticians and knew exactly what foods to eat and what not to eat. Too bad that knowing better doesn't always result in doing better. I didn't tell Mom, I didn't tell Dad, and I didn't tell Ahmed. I didn't tell my best friends. I didn't tell my shitty boyfriend, either. I just wrote one cryptic Facebook status and moved on with my life. It's not like anyone was going to find out. There weren't any obvious signs.

A month after I was diagnosed as diabetic so was Ahmed. He stayed in the hospital for almost a week. I sat with my family in Ahmed's hospital room and probably cried the entire time. (As I do.) It was hard to see my brother in the hospital, for one, but also I finally *was* devastated by diabetes. Just not my own. Ahmed was laid up in the hospital with tubes all over him, and I was sitting there in my cute little dress and purse getting away with not telling anyone. I felt horrible and guilty for being able to hide my diagnosis in a way that he, with diabetes on top of his weird blood disorder, couldn't. I just kept crying.

I didn't have to take insulin. I didn't have to prick myself to check my blood. I had a friend in college who was born diabetic and would make a huge show every few hours of testing her blood. She'd do it in front of everyone and then announce that she *had* to have some of whatever candy or chips anyone nearby was eating. I was thankful I didn't have to turn into her. My doctor was all like, "You can if you want, but you don't really need to." She was hella chill. She prescribed a drug to control my blood sugar. She told me that with diet and exercise, along with the medication, I could get my diabetes under control. She also wanted me to consider weight-loss surgery. She asked if I ever had. As if.

People think of weight-loss surgery as the easy way out. Maybe even I thought of it as the easy way out when I first started considering it more than ten years ago in between eating disorders. But then I failed as a candidate for the surgery and went back to puking. By the time I finally *did* stop throwing up, I was working at the phone sex office filled with plus-size women. Everyone around me was full grown and thriving . . . Oh, I guess you wouldn't call simulating blow jobs and wetting your hand to slap the other hand with it to fake the sound of a wet vagina *thriving* but, shit, I felt pretty accomplished back then! I was fine. Being among those beautiful, black, plus-size women helped me to find my own beauty and I am grateful for that. While I was there, I made friends with a girl who was bigger than I was and working toward her surgery. She already had a surgery date but was told to lose twenty pounds beforehand. Every day I'd watch her come into work from the gym, force herself to eat healthy foods she wasn't accustomed to eating, and leave work to hit the gym again before going home. I wasn't aware that you had to work that hard to get the surgery. Like if you're going to work that hard, why not just keep doing it instead of having surgery? I was young and stupid. I had yet to realize that whatever weight you are, your body wants to stay in the general area. Losing more than twenty pounds and keeping them off is extremely hard. My friend was going to take a month or two from work in order to heal from the surgery, but in the meantime, she had to take every and any shift possible in order to save up money to pay her bills during her time off. She also planned to take phone sex calls from home while she was recuperating. Yes! You can totally take phone sex calls from the comfort of your own home! Isn't this world amazing? I couldn't take that kind of time off and I couldn't take phone calls from home. I decided that surgery would be what I did when I had exhausted all other options.

Several years later my doctor was telling me I needed to start seriously considering the surgery. I had just started the first season of *The Big C,* my first TV series. When I wrapped that, I had to start filming *Tower Heist,* my first studio film. I didn't know when she thought I could take the time even to consider surgery, much less have it! My career was basically brand-new. And people liked me in this body. I might not have been that busy in a smaller body. Sure, there were the haters, fat-shamers, and plain old assholes who called me terrible names and then claimed that they were really just worried about my health. (Bullshit. No, they aren't. My parents are concerned for my health. *Fat-shamers* are just shitty, unhappy people, and they know it so they have to make fun of others in order to feel better about themselves.) But for the most part, people seemed fine with and even intrigued by my body. Probably because I was fine with it. I felt beautiful and, in fact, I was on *People* magazine's 50 Most Beautiful list that same year. While I knew that I was more than just my body—fat, skinny, or otherwise—I wasn't sure people who followed me would be aware of that. I was new to fame and I didn't yet know how not to give power to criticism and judgment. I couldn't even kick myself for not having had the surgery sooner, because if I had, I wouldn't have been right for the role of Precious and I'd probably still be on the phone sucking my cheeks to imitate the sound of a wet vagina. (There are SO many ways to fake a wet vagina! I'll give you a list later!) The surgery, when to do it, when not to do it, if I should or shouldn't do it, all felt like a catch-22. Damned if I do, diabetic if I don't. I decided again to give a really big push to lose weight naturally. It would take longer than surgery and I'd probably never get skinny, but I thought I could keep my weight in a manageable range. That's what I wanted. (I didn't want to be a skinny person. How would my skinny body support the weight of my huge ego?) I rehired my trainer. I started eating better. I got super into kale and shit! I started taking the stairs more. My weight went down and I was back to being prediabetic again. Then I got busy and distracted and hungry and lazy again. The weight came back. I went back to training and lost fifteen pounds or so again. Then I got busy again, but this time I was in New Orleans. It is impossible to have a bad meal in New Orleans! It is almost as impossible to find vegetables that aren't sautéed in butter among other delicious yet unhealthy things in New Orleans. I gained back all the weight and then some. No regrets. As I mentioned before, the food in NOLA is crazy delicious.

I finally made an appointment with the bariatric surgeon my doctor wanted me to see. I told no one. Again. No family, no friends. The receptionist told me about a seminar that I would have to go to before meeting the surgeon. A seminar with other people. Strangers. I was arguably one of the most famous fat people in America. That's a crazy category. Anyway, I didn't want to sit in a seminar full of strange people. I'm also super bad at saying things like "Hi! I'm famous. May I have special treatment now, please?" But I *needed* special treatment, so I had my doctor call and talk to the surgeon and explain why I should be able to skip the line. You bet your ass I went into that appointment with sunglasses and a wig. To be fair, that's like my normal daily wear. I'm never *not* wearing sunglasses and a wig. But that day I was extra sneaky about it. The surgeon asked me all the normal questions and weighed me to make sure I was a candidate for the procedure. He seemed really tired of me the whole time. Like he had much better things to do. I thought, *Perfect! This guy doesn't care who I am. He's just gonna be super professional about this and do his job.* But then, as we were finishing up the appointment, he asked, "So you're a singer or something?"

"No. Just an actor."

"You don't sing?"

"No."

"My nurse said you had an amazing voice. You don't sing?"

"Again, no."

"But you're on *Glee*. Don't you sing on *Glee*? They said you were on *Glee*."

Here's the thing. Amber Riley is on *Glee*. Amber Riley is not me. Amber is black, young, and plus-size. Amber is *still* not me. We don't even look alike. No matter the many labels we may share, she and I remain two separate people. Amber happens to be one of my really good friends. I'm talking grown-up sleepovers, fixing each other plates, flying out to birthday celebrations, and borrowing each other's wigs. She's my homie.

I will still be incredibly offended if anyone confuses one of us for the other. Not because I don't want to be compared to her and her greatness, but because it's racist. Anyway, this surgeon was now basically dead to me. I didn't want him to do my surgery. I was actually still figuring out if I wanted it at all, but I knew this guy wasn't the guy for me. He should've stopped asking after the first or second no. I was already a ball of anxiety about the procedure. I was alone. I hadn't discussed it with anyone for privacy reasons, and to know that the staff there was talking and giggling about me, and not even the right me, turned me off. The surgeon told me that I would have to pass the psychological evaluation before going any further.

Good, I thought. *I'll just go ahead and fail my evaluation like before and then I won't have to do any of this.*

Surprise! I passed! Seriously. I was not planning on passing. I told the truth about DBT therapy and the eating disorders. Sure, by now it had all happened almost ten years ago, but I didn't realize that I would present the perfect picture of mental health. Now I had a decision to make. Move forward with someone I was uncomfortable with, find another surgeon, or just get super serious about losing weight naturally again.

After straight-up napping on it for a month, I chose option C. I took a few months off to eat whatever I wanted, and then I got super into training. It truly felt like my last chance. I could almost feel sickness one step behind me. Maybe even death. Ugh! That's sooo dramatic! But it might have been true. Five years of secretly living with diabetes comfortably was starting to feel weird. I was afraid I couldn't keep it up for much longer. Ahmed had ended up in the hospital again. Mom was now sick with some kind of infection and was dropping weight really quickly. When she'd first started slimming down after a lifetime of being heavy, she took it as a blessing. She started to worry a little later. She told me she'd been hitting the gym and eating grapefruit and stuff. I was suspicious since I never saw her eating anything but Oreos and boiled eggs. I had no idea she was sick. I was out of town a lot and she just didn't tell me. Even when she ended up in the hospital, she was there a whole day before a friend of hers called to tell me. See where I get it? Everyone I loved was getting sick from a lifetime of eating like a POW survivor. My secret and I were probably running out of time.

The story of how I got to the bariatric department of UCLA Medical Center is long and filled with uninteresting twists, so I'll spare you. I'm just glad I did. I wanted the surgery, and for the first time, I *knew* it. I realized that after eleven years of saying, "Surgery will be the last resort," I was finally here. At my last resort. Another huge difference that let me know I was serious this time was that I told my favorite friend, Kia, I had an appointment to see some doctors about the possibility of weight-loss surgery.

"Okay. You know I don't like doctors and hospitals, so tell me when our appointment is so that I can go pray and meditate on it before we go."

"'Our'? 'We'? Nah. You don't have to come with me," I told her. She looked at me like I was stupid and rolled her eyes.

"Girl, let me go light this incense and meditate on *our* appointment," she said, leaving the room. She was going with me. End of discussion. No matter how many times I insisted she could stay home or in the car or go to brunch during my appointment, she sat right next to me in that doctor's office at UCLA Medical. I am forever grateful she didn't listen to me.

The team at UCLA Medical is amazing! They were so cool and kind while explaining things to Kia and me. My surgeon said I'd have laparoscopic bariatric surgery. They'd go in, cut my stomach in half, sew it up, and pull what they took out of there. I almost asked if I could take it home with me in a jar, but I figured that was kind of weird. This surgery would reduce my stomach and limit my hunger and capacity to eat. After three weeks, my brain chemistry would change and I'd want to eat healthier. The surgeon said that the medical profession didn't know exactly why that happens due to this surgery, but it does. Whatever! I'll take it! *Laparoscopic* is kind of a scary word. I think it means that the surgery is somehow done with lasers. Fancy. Everything at the hospital was so fancy. I had an appointment before surgery with four different people, two surgeons, another doctor, and a dietician. When I arrived, there was a greeter waiting to take me up to the medical suite where my appointments were. Instead of sitting in the waiting room, I was ushered into an exam room. I stayed there for every single appointment and each doctor came to me. That's fucking service! I've never seen such a thing. As much as I sometimes complain about being so recognizable, I was very grateful for this privacy and for these people making sure I could get the surgery and heal and be back at work ASAP.

The scariest part about all of this—more than the two-to-three-night hospital stay, more than the lasers beaming into my stomach, more than having to rely on everyone keeping my secret—was going back to work. The surgeons said that I would lose weight really fast at first. I would be shooting season three of *Empire* in three months. I had a very established body in seasons one and two. I knew I'd already look different for the first episode and that by the last show of the season I might be completely unrecognizable. Viewers would notice. Should the writers address it in the script? Wasn't I supposed to give the show's creators a heads-up that I was thinking about the procedure? How could I do this to them? Was I a horrible person? What about the costume department? I was going to start shrinking during production. Just when they thought they had my size, it would go down and they'd be foiled again. They're all great people! Why would I do this to them? Shouldn't I take the time to consider what I was doing to the show?

"No," Kia said.

Just no. Kia is THE BEST! She's right. This is my body! *Mine.* Yes, I had a job, several jobs, but my number-one job was to make sure that I was healthy. That I was alive. Explaining my changing body to viewers, the costumes fitting—that was all someone else's job. My cast and crew loved and supported me, and I was sure the inconvenience of my morphing body would be outweighed by the pride they'd feel for my handling my own shit and getting healthy by any means necessary. Or . . . maybe the surgery wouldn't be a success. Maybe I wouldn't lose any weight at all. Maybe everything would stay the same. Maybe there'd be nothing but my health to worry about. Forever.

My appointment with the bariatric team was on April 7. My surgery was set for May 9. That's what the professionals call "fast as fuck." I had to lose ten pounds at least before the surgery to help the laser get to my stomach. I didn't super know what that meant. I just got my ass in gear. Ten pounds is actually pretty easy for me to lose. If that's all I need to do. Unfortunately, I had a million things to do, so Kia helped me find and hire a private chef. That's hella fancy, y'all! Kia also found a boxing trainer to help me work out. After a few weeks of this regime on top of working at all kinds of stressful things that I usually stress-eat through, I was exhausted! I couldn't wait for the surgery. It was going to be nice to veg out for a day or two.

On my birthday I had Popeye's chicken and biscuits, fries, and a Dr Pepper. Later that day, I was at a wedding so I drank plenty of champagne and tequilas with lime. I was going to miss food and booze. After surgery, I would be on a liquid diet for three weeks as my new stomach would not be able to handle much. Then my brain would tell me to crave salad instead of pizza . . . allegedly. My lifelong relationship with food had to change. This was sadder than I thought it would be. The way I lived, the way I thought, the way I ate, the things I did with my friends and family, the way I watched TV, the way I self-soothed and celebrated had to change. I would have to do all of those things without food. I didn't know how, but it would kill me if I didn't figure it out.

The day before the surgery was the beginning of the liquid diet. Kia vowed to do it with me. I loafed around all day reading a script that Nick Cannon had written for me. The character was a plus-size girl who is called fat ass and hippo. I thought how glad I'd be when my body was no longer mentioned in script ideas for me. "My body is not a character description." My good friend Amber Riley once said that. I would call Nick in a few days and have him remove those names. Boy, would he be pissed by the time we shot the movie. I called my mom but didn't share anything about the operation, and then Kia and I went to bed pretty early. We had to be at the hospital at 3 a.m. the next morning. In the middle of the night, I woke up, showered, and packed a small bag for my hospital stay. Before getting in the car, Kia anointed my head with oil and we prayed together for a successful surgery. I was filled with butterflies but kept imagining them being shot down with the surgeon's lasers. We listened to the radio and sang along on the way to UCLA. We were both scared. I was glad to have someone to be scared with. When we got to the hospital, we checked in; I changed into the hospital gown, took two selfies, and waited for the doctors. They came and I reminded them that I needed to make it out of surgery. "Do everything you can to keep me alive. Even if you have to kill someone else, do it. I *have* to survive!" My surgeon chuckled and said I'd be fine. I believed him. I worried a little about no one in my family knowing I was having the surgery. If I died during the procedure, they'd not only be shocked and upset, they'd be pissed at Kia! That's a lot of pressure to put on one person. She calmly sat with me, and reminded me to have "faith over fear," and helped me breathe through my panic. Soon I was in the operating room, and after what seemed like even sooner, I was in recovery drifting in and out of consciousness.

Kia was scared to see me afterward, weak in a hospital bed. But she got herself together and came back to the hospital later that day, and the first thing I said to her as I put my hands on my hips while lying in the bed was "Bitch! Do I look skinny? It's me! Gabby! You recognize me?" Two days later she picked me up and we went back to our rental house. I had three days' worth of texts and work e-mails and requirements from people who had no idea that I had just had surgery. I was tired. My stomach was trembling and sending waves of pain through my entire body. I had oxycodone for the pain, but it made me sleepy and spaced-out. The first few nights, I would wake up at 4:20 a.m. on the dot. I'd have to get up and take the oxy just to get back to sleep. Kia made me sleep with my door open, and every time she heard me shuffling, she'd scream, "You OKAY?! You takin' drugs?!" She watched me like a hawk and made me drink all my dumb liquids even though I wasn't hungry. To actually lift something to my mouth to drink or eat felt like a huge hassle. Maybe it was my brain talking, but I was not interested in eating. A part of me would have loved five minutes alone with a tray of lasagna. I *wanted* it. I didn't *need* it. The biggest obstacle between what I wanted and what I needed was my new stomach. I was very sad about all of my food needing to be wet for the first three weeks after surgery. (But I can't tell you how exciting it was afterward to have my first softly scrambled egg. *Really* fucking exciting!) All I did was think about food and fantasize about my new body. Kia vowed to do the liquid diet with me, but she started to get spacey and headachy, so I told her to start eating actual food. She swore she wouldn't and I swore I'd be fine. She started eating kale and cauliflower, and I immediately called her a traitor. I was totally kidding. It actually made me feel better to yell at her about eating when I couldn't. I just liked yelling and talking about food. Shit. That's weird. Is that who I am now? Is this how I self-soothe?

A couple of weeks after surgery I had to go to an *Empire* screening and a panel for Emmy voters. I was super excited to get my hair and makeup done and get out of the house! As I walked down the red carpet, I could already feel the difference in my weight. I usually sweat on red carpets because of nervousness and wearing heels. I stayed completely dry, and my feet didn't even hurt. I was still spaced-out because of my liquid diet, but I had much more red carpet endurance than I usually would. In the holding area, there were food and drinks. Delicious-looking sandwiches, fruit platters, crudités, and all the wine and vodka I wanted . . . but I *didn't* want it. Everyone said I looked great and that I was glowing. Whatever. Kia had been saying that when I was still in the hospital, but I didn't think anyone else would. Right before we went onstage, I slipped into the bathroom to check my makeup. I saw myself in the mirror. Or *not* me in the mirror. I hadn't seen it before but now I could. I had lost quite a bit of weight. My face was thinner. My eyes seemed bigger. Yes, I had makeup on, but I was also, in fact, glowing. I saw what I looked like and I was scared. Really scared. It was less than two weeks after surgery. What would I look like in the next two weeks? In the next month? In the next year? Who would I look like then?

When I say that I'm beautiful, I don't say it so someone will clap and think I'm brave. I'm not doing it so that someone will comment on how confident I am. I don't say it with ego and I don't say it defensively. I don't say it meaning that people who look like me are better than people who look like you. I say it because I believe it. I've earned every centimeter of my beauty. It has taken me years to realize that what I was born with, what was shaped, the mold it took, is all beautiful. I did not get this surgery to be beautiful. I did it so that I can walk around comfortably in heels. I want to do a cartwheel. I want not to be in pain every time I walk up a flight of stairs. I want to stop worrying about losing my toes.

I know I'm beautiful in my current face *and* my current body. What I don't know about is the next body. The next face. I admit, I hope to God I don't get skinny. If I could lose enough to just be a little chubby, I'll be over the moon! I don't know what that will look like, my new face, my new body. Will I still be beautiful then? *Shiiiiit.* Probably. My beauty doesn't come from a mirror. Never has and never will.

18

NEXT

Do you expect me to be satisfied with a hashtag?
— Peaches, *The Tale of Four*

THIS IS BARRASSING, BUT WHEN I was a teenager, I used to write fan fiction about the pop group NSYNC. It's what I did instead of homework or class work. It's the reason, other than skipping gym, I had to work so hard to graduate. I would spend most days incessantly writing down my creeptastic fantasies about Justin, JC, Chris, Joey, and Lance in composition notebooks. I'd write about Crystal and me being adopted by NSYNC after sneaking onto their tour bus, getting caught, and going on the rest of their world tour with them. (What? Like that can't happen?) A lot of times I wrote about being friends or even enemies (for drama!) with them in a reality (Ha! *Reality?* What's that?!) where they weren't famous at all and we were all in high school together. My friends, classmates, and teachers wanted to know what I was always writing. Because my bedroom kept filling up with more and more notebooks, my family suspected I was up to something other than just a what-I-did-today diary. The most interesting thing I did back then was cut class to sit by myself in the bathroom until math was over or head home to watch *The Kids in the Hall* reruns. My life has never been interesting enough to record at length. Until now (wink).

No one but Crystal knew that I was, in fact, writing a TV show starring a boy band (one I knew most intimately from daily Internet searching in my eighth-period computer class). Obviously. GOD, I'M SO EMBARRASSED! WHY CAN'T I STOP MYSELF FROM ADMITTING THIS! Anyway, every day I'd write a new episode of the show. After about six months of writing, I'd end the show, take a day off, and then start writing an entirely new show with the same cast, a different story line, and a different personality for each cast member. I'd go from being a senior in a performing-arts high school who insists on being a virgin until marriage to being a widowed, single mom down on her luck in Las Vegas who becomes a prostitute in the next season. If this sounds familiar to you, yes, I was doing then what Ryan Murphy does with *American Horror Story* today, which makes the fact that I eventually joined the cast of *American Horror Story* so weird. Life is so weird, you guys!

Anyway, this went on for about seven years. I wrote thirteen seasons. That's what I did when I couldn't afford therapy. I wrote. If I had a bad day, I wrote myself a better day. If a cute guy just wanted to be my friend, I'd write about two men fighting over me even though neither of them were good enough for me. Writing helped me to process what was going on inside me and around me. I created characters who dealt with depression, eating disorders, rejection. When I started my phone sex job in real life, I wrote a season about prostitutes and strippers. The members of NSYNC were my scaffolding, but I didn't *know* them. I *knew* me. The stories were about me. I mean, please, go ahead and make fun of me. I still have the notebooks and they are truly my secret shame. To this day, the only person who has ever read what I wrote is Crystal.

When it turned out years later that several people including agents and editors thought I could write a book, I froze! I was some fat nobody who now starred in a film but was still often treated like a fat nobody. How could I write a book about that? How would my mom and dad look on the page to people who didn't know and love them? How would Ahmed look? My friends, my bosses, my coworkers? If I told the truth about foster care, Dad's second wife, my parents ignoring my depression, phone sex, Hollywood—wasn't someone bound to get hurt? Or would it just be me? Never mind getting hurt, would I curl up and *die* of embarrassment from all I'd admitted about myself? I was sure everyone was completely wrong about me and whatever book they thought I'd write.

Today, obviously, I wrote this book. You just read it. The way it happened was . . . I just wrote the truth, and it made me feel better. So I wrote more. I felt even better. After two years of telling the truth on the page, as I know it, I've written an entire book that has helped reshape my view on life, my work, my body, my family, and, most important, myself. I used to think celebrities wrote books for the money or to squeeze a few more seconds out of their fifteen minutes of fame. Now

I know that many people in general, not just celebrities, write about their own lives to find purpose for pain. I get it, man. Writing this book has sent me straight into the arms (couch) of my therapist, but it has also allowed me to see people who have hurt me as just that. *People.* The hurt is no longer part of the equation. People. Just like me. I'm a person who has been hurt, but I'm also a person who *has* hurt. When I first started writing more than two years ago, I had cut my father out of my life entirely. Now I've found a way to forgive him enough to listen to him bore me to death about real estate in Senegal. (Seriously. He is hella into that shit and talked to me about it for twenty whole minutes while I said, *"Mmhmm . . . Oh? . . . Wow . . . Cool,"* in two-minute intervals two days ago.) Any money I make or seconds I add to my fifteen minutes of fame by writing this book mean nothing compared to the peace of mind I get from being happy and settled in my heart about my family. I love them dearly even if the stories in this book prevent you from being able to do the same. What's great is that my mom keeps saying she's fine with anything I write as long as it's the truth. She also said she probably wouldn't be reading my book, though. That's fine, too. (OH! And by the way, neither of my parents or Ahmed knows that I was a phone sex operator, so you guys be cool! I can't afford to get grounded right now.)

No one could have told me that I'd ever write a book, and no one could have told me I'd ever direct a film. Except a psychic! Actually, this one was fancy and called himself a "spiritual advisor." Either way, I was too scared and lazy to ask him to elaborate. I was sure he was just assuming that I, being an actor, was interested in directing someday. But back then he was dead wrong. I had zero interest in directing. My first director, Lee Daniels, knows exactly what he wants and how to get it. He doesn't accept anything less than what he asks for. I watched him very carefully on set. I took in every bit of his process, and said, "Nope!" I didn't want the responsibility. I didn't think I could care about anything enough to fight for it the way I'd seen Lee and every other director I'd ever worked with fight for what they wanted to say with their work. Me, a director? The boss of a movie? I didn't want to be the boss. What if I failed? What if I wasn't as good as Lee Daniels? Or as good as anybody? That would be horrible. Even as a phone sex operator, while I wasn't content to sit at a desk moaning into a phone my whole life, I never wanted to be the boss of the entire company. Somewhere in the middle without a spotlight or too much responsibility would've been all I needed. There's no fear in the middle.

But that was six years ago.

I directed my first film, *The Tale of Four*, during the summer of 2016 and immediately submitted it to film festivals. The film is an adaptation of the Nina Simone song called "Four Women" about four strong black women from four distinct worlds: an abused woman, a woman of mixed race, a woman called Sweet Thing who uses the power of her sexuality, and a tough, bitter woman whose life "has been too rough." My producing partner Kia (you know her!) came up with the idea a few years ago, and we built an entire world around those women.

Well, thank God I was a creepy fat kid, cuz it has made for an interesting adulthood! Out of really nowhere, Shatterbox, an offshoot of Refinery29, offered me the chance to direct any short film I chose. I could've said no. I had just finished a season of *Empire,* was writing this book, and secretly considering surgery before going back to work on *Empire*. I had only months to get the entire film done. Also, I'd never directed *traffic*. How would I direct actors and a crew of people looking to me for answers? I wanted to say no. No made the most sense. But writing this book had reminded me that my life has been filled with nos from other people. The only time something got interesting in my life was when someone said yes.

I said yes, but the film needed to be Kia's, too. Even if I couldn't yet believe 100 percent in my own voice when it came to directing a film, I believed in hers. Kia has known she wanted to be a filmmaker for most of her life. She went to college for it. She'd already directed her own shorts. When I was a twenty-four-year-old phone sex worker who'd tripped into a starring film role, I envied her tenacity. She did exactly what she wanted to do instead of what she felt she *had* to do. Like my mom. Her job was a fantasy job . . . on purpose. When I was given the chance to make my own film, I knew I needed Kia.

I asked her if I could direct the film and told her that I would fight to hire her as producer. Kia was skeptical at first. Handing over this film idea that she had held on to for years wasn't easy for her. We both worried that Refinery29 would police us with rules and veto our ideas and change the story completely on us. That didn't happen. At our first production meeting we found out who the actual bosses were. Turns out, it was Kia and I. We were in charge.

After hiring Kia as creator and producer of our film, I brought on super producer Lisa Cortes to be a part of our team. Lisa has produced films with Lee Daniels for years. She produced *Precious* and never ceased to amaze me with her ability to be a lovely, smart problem solver who expresses her wants and vision without apology. A woman who doesn't apologize for her very existence on Earth is rare, and that's what I wanted for myself. I would carefully listen to every word she said on set. Hiring her for my first film was a great decision. I needed a whip-smart woman in our corner to fight for Kia's and my voice in case we couldn't do it on our own.

We didn't yet realize our own strength.

Kia was in charge of assembling our crew. She set up interviews for me with assistant directors and camera operators. My friend and mentor Victoria Mahoney, an actress turned director who had hired me for my second film role, told me the assistant directors I'd be interviewing would most likely be men and to watch for those who seemed ready to undermine me. The first assistant director I met was a man who wanted the job, assumed he had it, and kept commenting during the interview how smart I was. But not in a good way. Every time I said anything that showed I knew what I was doing, he said, "Oh . . . so you're smart, huh?" Ladies! You *know* what I'm talking about, right? Hell, no. Not on MY set! I hired a very smart and serious assistant director who had done some documentary work I liked. My director of photography had worked on projects I admired, too, and he had a very Zen-like, calm demeanor. In fact, there are photos of him on our set standing on his head. (Buddhist monks do that, right? No? They don't? They *should*.) Both of these men became my pillars of support. Both of them listened patiently to all of my thoughts and concerns. Neither of them ever said no to me. Neither ever tried to be louder than I was. They both taught me so much and allowed me to make my film the way I wanted.

No one on our crew was there to get rich, which would've been impossible. We had champagne dreams for our beer-budget film. Some of our crew belonged to unions that wouldn't let them work without proper compensation. So they changed their names for us and were paid much less than they were worth. Just because they believed in us. From our actors to hair and makeup to producers, camera operators, and set photographers — we had friends, family, and allies in every department of this film who all happened to be talented, award-winning professionals. Every time I started to feel overwhelmed or nervous, I'd look up in any direction and see my friends there for me — and it would immediately calm me down. That was the real joy. Being surrounded by people who all were there to support me and what we wanted to say with our film.

What did we want to say? The film takes place in an urban setting. Our Aunt Sarah, Simone's long-suffering woman, is raising children who aren't hers and mourning the loss of her husband and sister. We portray Saffronia, a mixed-race teenager raised by a single mother, being bullied on her way home from school and then again on the web. (Fucking Millennials! I'm kidding. You're probably reading this book right now. Hi! Snapchat is so lit, right?) Sweet Thing is an artist who is sleeping with a married man. And then there's Peaches. Peaches is a video blogger who sits in front of a shrine to her dead son made up of his medals of achievement, college graduation pictures, and diploma; she is making a vlog update after more than a year of fighting for justice for her son, who was killed by a police officer.

I'm a black woman. Surprise! I don't want to get into a conversation about race relations, being compliant around police officers, or #AllLives vs. #BlueLives vs. #BlackLivesMatter. Frankly, that conversation feels like it's too big and important to have in a book where I talk about using my imagination to blow creeps over the phone and writing fan fiction featuring NSYNC. It's also too big a conversation to have on Twitter (as we Millennials do). Every time I tweet something like "Why are police so quick to shoot down and kill unarmed black men when their hands are clearly in the air?" I get about a hundred tweets from eggs or profile pictures of Trump or the Confederate flag calling me a monkey or a fat nigger. Tweets telling me to go back to Africa (according to my dad, I have a lovely home in Senegal, so being told to go back there is actually a great vacation suggestion; thanks, racist!) or telling me that I should be grateful that my people were saved from Africa and brought here in the first place. I get tweets about how black people kill one another all the time so—so what if *police* kill them? No, Twitter may not be the right place for this conversation. But I don't have the privilege of pretending I'm not concerned about the target that seems to be tattooed on the backs of people who look like me or that I am not absolutely terrified. Not for myself, for all of the black men in my life. For Ahmed. For my younger brothers, Malick and Abdul. All three of my brothers are gentle giants who stand over six feet tall. Abdul, who is twenty-two years old now, has special needs and speaks with a very pronounced stutter. The idea of him walking around Brooklyn by himself and being perceived as a threat by the police and not being able to talk his way out of a standoff terrifies me. I can't say that on Twitter, so I had to find a way to say it in my film.

When it came to Peaches's story, it was an extra-emotional day on set. For one, I cast my real-life cousin Sean to play Peaches's murdered son. Sean is six-foot-four, kind, and harmless. He came in for photography the day before his wedding. He's three years younger than I am, and no matter how much he towers over me, he will always be my nerdy little cousin. Directing our actress, Aisha Hinds, to cry over his photograph was harder than I thought. I directed the entire day with tears streaming down my face, but it was worth it to convey our message. Please see my humanity before you kill me.

With every role I play in film or television, my goal is to bring life and humanity to the character. To lose myself and dive into someone else's space and world. With my own work, like this book and my film, I don't have a character to hide behind. I wrote this! These are my experiences, thoughts, and emotions. If someone reads this book and decides that I'm a bad person, I can't say, "Oh, you just don't like Becky from *Empire* or Andrea from *The Big C*." Nope. It's Gabby from Gabourey who that person doesn't like. If someone doesn't like my film, it's just me here—my art, my opinion. (Directing is just a matter of opinion. I learned that from my assistant director Marcus.)

I knew that if I wrote a book or directed a film I would be on my own without anything to hide behind. That's why I didn't want to do it. Fear. But here we are five or so years later, and the fear is gone. I'm standing by myself in front of the entire world with my book under one arm and my film under the other. Most of my secrets, most of my shames and fears, are written into them. My humanity is written into them, too, and I actually don't care if someone doesn't like it. That's just an opinion. It won't ever make me any less human.

Thank you for reading.

P.S. Yes, it is *hella* awkward whenever I run into anyone from NSYNC. They never want to make out with me like in my soap operas. Rude.

ACKNOWLEDGMENTS

There are many names swirling around my head to thank or acknowledge concerning this book. I would love to brag that I wrote this book all by myself — and I do and will continue to do so — but I certainly couldn't have done it without the push of several people I am grateful to know.

Working backward, I have to first thank Deanne Urmy of Houghton Mifflin Harcourt, my editor, whom I trusted most because she knows how to interrupt me and stop me from talking. I don't mean that in a passive-aggressive "she's always interrupting me" way because I'm so grateful for it. I tend to talk too much, tell too much of the story and then the back-story and then the *back* backstory. It's too much and the first story, the only interesting part, gets lost. Deanne always keeps me on track while protecting the true story. It is a gift to be shut up by you, Deanne. When I first met Deanne, I noted that she looked smart and that everyone at HMH seemed bright. I soon found out that Deanne was even smarter than she looked that day. A brilliant woman I'm blessed to have in my corner.

Thank you, Deanne. Also, she knows that when I say "Oh, yeah, I'm almost done with this chapter; I'll send it to you by Friday" that I am most certainly lying and I mean Friday of next month. Thank you for never calling my bluff.

Becky Sweren, who was my editor before HMH, helped me so much. She carved every single one of my ramblings into a solid story, sometimes taking three different chapters and making them one as if she were a literary Frankenstein. Just as brilliantly, she could take one chapter and turn them into three. This gave me so much freedom! I felt as if I could write as much or as little as I wanted but that it was all valuable in some way so that even if I didn't think the paragraphs and themes would somehow meet each other Becky would find the links and make sure they were consistent. Clearly, this book would've just been a pile of Post-it notes with crudely drawn emojis and tearstains on them if she hadn't wrangled my rants and tweets together to make the manuscript. Thank you.

David Kuhn, my literary agent, is a fancy man in a fancy hat who could sell snow to an Eskimo. He first had to sell me on the idea that maybe I had a book in me. Then he had to sell me on *sharing* the possible book in me as I was sure it was all a dark mess. I'm glad he convinced me. My dark mess didn't seem so dark or messy on the page, and my heart felt lighter. I didn't expect that. Then he sold the living shit out of those not so dark and not so messy pages. I couldn't be happier. Thank you, David, for helping me to bleed. In a good way.

Jill Kaplan is my manager and friend, and she has never let me be complacent about one thing. She has helped to usher me around all of the different facets of my career and of who I am as a person. From film actor to TV actor to writer to director. Even when I'm not convinced I'm smart enough to do any of these things, she always keeps me moving in directions I'd never think of just by saying, "But, Gab . . . why *not* you? You can do that." *We* can do that. Thank you, Jill.

Kathy Najimy. Thank you. You gave me the space and opportunity to write anything that I wanted. ANYTHING! I wrote an eight-page essay about cookies for you that somehow turned into a book. An entire gotdamned book! How did this happen? Forever, you'll either be mistaken for a nun or a witch, and I will forever be convinced of your power, as clearly you are both!

Though I suspect none of them will ever read this book as they already know these stories, I have to thank my parents and my older brother. Not just because I talk lots of shit about them but because I respect and love them. Writing about them has helped me to see them as they actually are. Human. There were times I didn't want to write about my mom because I'd be pissed with her about one thing or another so I would put off a certain story for weeks. Sometimes months. But when I started to write, I'd always somehow end up on the subject of her. I'd have no choice but to see her sacrifices, her pain, and her glory. My story wouldn't be if not for her story, and I couldn't ignore that. The same could be said for my father, who I've been mad at since childhood. I had to write this story and part of his story to see his humanity and get relief from my anger. I didn't even know that this was something I wanted, but I'm glad I have it. He is just a person. I know that now. I forgive both of my parents for not being the superheroes I was convinced they were. My brother Ahmed, who survived my childhood right along with me, has been a shining example of what your heart can be if you choose love over anger. I'm glad he did that even if I couldn't figure out how to do it for myself.

Thank you to my friends, my chosen family who read portions of my book earlier than anyone else. You all let me read unfinished chapters to you that revealed more about me than I was ready to tell. You patiently listened and gave me notes and asked me if I was sure I was ready to tell *that* story or *this* truth. You're all so wonderful, and I appreciate you all so much, and every time you wanted to hang out and I said I was writing, I was lying. I just wanted to stay home and watch *Martin* reruns and eat Funyuns in my underwear. But you'll forgive me for my lies because you're the best people in the world. Thank you also for getting me out of the house when I was actually writing and needed a mental break. There were plenty of late-night trips to Burger King or Portillo's, dance breaks, movie nights, and talks over tea that saved me from drowning in the word soup of my brain. JohnGray, Cass, Danie, Dana, Kia, Jussie, thank you for all of your love.

Thank you to Gbenga Akinnagbe and his beautiful ENITAN furniture for lending me a gorgeous couch for my book's photo shoot. I really felt like a boss when that couch showed up!

Lastly, a shout-out to my therapist. Get dat money, gurl.